ENGLISH SPELLING
AND
SPELLING REFORM

BY
THOMAS R. LOUNSBURY, LL.D., L.H.D.
Emeritus Professor of English
in Yale University

GREENWOOD PRESS, PUBLISHERS
WESTPORT, CONNECTICUT

C

Δ
4 21·52

LOU

Originally published in 1909
by Harper & Brothers, New York

First Greenwood Reprinting 1970

Library of Congress Catalogue Card Number 74-109774

SBN 8371-4264-4

Printed in the United States of America

TO

BRANDER MATTHEWS

AS A TRIBUTE TO A FELLOW-COMBATANT IN
A COMMON CAUSE, AND A TESTIMONIAL OF
THE LONG-CONTINUED FRIENDSHIP OF YEARS

CONTENTS

PREFACE

THE main ideas underlying the treatment here found of English orthography were embodied in an article which appeared in the *Atlantic Monthly* for June, 1907. The title it there bore was "Confessions of a Spelling Reformer." This it was the original intention to give to the present work. But with the changes which were required in recasting the article upon which it was based, with the great expansion of many of the points considered in it, more than all with the extension of its scope so as to include many new topics, the personal element which had characterized it none too prominently in the first place sank into almost complete insignificance. Hence followed the inappropriateness of the title. Here, accordingly, it has been confined to the opening chapter, and for it has been substituted that which the volume now bears.

As published in the magazine, the article referred to was of a length so unconscionable that

PREFACE

I have always been confident that the editor, however carefully he concealed his feelings, groaned inwardly at the space he obliged himself to give up to it. Still, long as it was, much which had been prepared for it was cut out before transmission. It was felt that there is a point beyond which the patience of the most long-suffering of editors will not stretch. A few passages which were then omitted were later made to do service in a presidential address given at the annual meeting of the Simplified Spelling Board. These have been restored here, though in a much enlarged form, to their old place. With them also has been reinstated a good deal of other matter which had been struck out before the article was forwarded for publication. I have also made use of several paragraphs which had appeared a number of years ago in contributions to the *Century Magazine*. In addition, it is to be said that one whole chapter in the volume has been printed before, though very much abbreviated, in *Harper's Magazine*. But in spite of the extent to which I have drawn upon matter previously published, fully two-thirds of the contents of the present treatise has never up to this time appeared in print. This is true in particular of what in my own eyes is the most important chapter in the book—that on the Orthographic Situation.

The subject of spelling reform is not, strictly speaking, a soul-stirring one, nor is any possible treatment of it likely to contribute to the gayety of nations. If any of the chapters contained in the present volume be of the slightest interest in itself, that on the orthographic situation is assuredly not the one. On the other hand, if there be anything of value in the work, that same chapter has, as I look at it, far the most value. There is in it, indeed, nothing original. The numerous facts it contains are to be found scattered up and down the pages of various volumes—particularly in the introductions to the larger dictionaries, and in orthographic and orthoepic essays produced at various periods. But so far as I know, this is the first attempt ever made to collect and combine and, above all, to put in a form, easily comprehensible by the general reader, the widely scattered facts which go to show the precise character and characteristics of English orthography, and to bring out with distinctness the real nature of the deep-seated disease under which it labors.

At all events, whether or not I have been anticipated in the presentation of these facts, such knowledge of them as can be gained from this volume or from some better source is essential to the comprehension of the subject or to any proper consideration of it. Designedly and avowedly incomplete as is the survey of the subject here taken, it is sufficiently detailed to give any one who cares to understand it a fair degree of familiarity with the situation which confronts him who sets out to effect a genuine and not a spurious reform. It is furthermore sufficient to give him a fair conception of the sort of work that will have to be done before the anarchy which now prevails in our spelling can give way to even the semblance of order.

Assuredly there was ample need of a work of this sort being prepared, and the only regret that need be entertained is that it has not fallen to some one better equipped than myself to prepare it. For I reiterate in this preface what I have said in the body of the work itself: that there is no one subject upon which men, whether presumably or really intelligent, are in a state of more hopeless, helpless ignorance than upon that of the nature and history of English orthography. No serious student of it can read the articles which appear in newspapers, the communications sent to them, or the elaborate

PREFACE

essays found in periodicals, without being struck by the more than Egyptian darkness which prevails. In nearly every one of these mistakes of fact not merely exist but abound. Most of the assertions made lack even that decent degree of probability which belongs to respectable fiction. Even in the very few cases where the facts are correct, the inferences drawn from them are utterly erroneous and misleading. Many of these articles, too, contain mistakes of apprehension so gross that one comes to feel that in the discussion of this particular subject the limits of human incapacity to understand the simplest assertion have been reached. Statements of this sort will be resented with all the venomousness of anonymous personal vituperation. They have not been made, however, without full examination of scores and scores of articles which have come out in opposition to spelling reform. No difficulty will be found, if the occasion demands, to substantiate their correctness beyond the shadow of a doubt.

The various chapters contained in this volume follow one another in logical sequence. But I have also sought to make each of them, in a way, independent of the others, and therefore complete in itself. This has necessitated, in a very few cases, the repetition of statements im-

xi

portant only for the immediate understanding of the particular subject. I may venture to add that I have taken great pains to make the numerous details scattered through the volume absolutely correct, so that he who quarrels with the conclusions reached may have no cause to question the facts upon which they are based. If in the immense mass of these found here I have made anywhere a slip, I shall be grateful for the detection of it, and none the less so if it come from the most hostile source. In this subject it is the exact truth of which we are in pursuit, and a real though not a fancied exposure of error is to be welcomed gladly.

The movement now going on for the simplification of English spelling has in the few years of its existence attained a success which has never been even remotely approached by any similar attempt in the past. This has been due, in part, to the fact that an effort for reform has for the first time had behind it the support of an organized propaganda. Previous undertakings of the sort have been mainly the work of individuals. It has likewise been due, in part, to the general spread of knowledge as to the nature and history of words belonging to our speech and the changes of form they have undergone. Something also is due to the growing dissatisfaction, a consequence of this increase of intelligence, with the anomalies and absurdities of the present spelling, and the loss of time and labor, the waste of money, and the mental injury which the acquisition of these perverse and perverted forms involves. In our country, also, this feeling of dissatisfaction has been strengthened by the consideration that something must be done to remove from the path of that mighty army of foreigners landing yearly upon our shores the greatest of the stumbling-blocks in the way of the acquisition of the English language, necessary as the knowledge of it is to any comprehension by them of the laws and institutions and political ideas of the land they are henceforth to make their home.

Flourishing as the present movement assuredly is, it of course may fail ultimately, as have several which have preceded it. It certainly will fail if the propaganda does not continue to be vigorously pressed. It will fail if proposals are adopted and methods are followed which, while pleasing sciolists, do not recommend themselves to scholars. That experiment has been too often tried to leave us in any doubt as to the result. But whatever be the success or failure which may attend the present movement, none the less am I confident that the

PREFACE

English race will not be content to sit down forever with a system of spelling which has nothing to recommend it but custom and prejudice, nothing to defend it but ignorance, nothing but superstition to make it an object of veneration. An orthography which defies the main object for which orthography was created cannot continue, with the advance of knowledge, to be endured forever; for speaking with absolute reverence, it can be said of it that, not being of God, it cannot stand.

ENGLISH SPELLING AND
SPELLING REFORM

ENGLISH SPELLING AND SPELLING REFORM

CHAPTER I

CONFESSIONS OF A SPELLING REFORMER

IT was my fortune in 1906 to be wandering
in lands where English is not spoken, when
the President of the United States issued his
famous order in regard to spelling. Little,
therefore, of the comment it occasioned met my
eyes, either at the time or long after; little of
the clamor it excited reached my ears. But
after my return to my own country I had the
opportunity to look over no small number of
the productions which came out in opposition
to it or in criticism of it, whether they appeared
in the form of reported interviews with prominent persons, of leaders in newspapers or letters
to them, or of elaborate articles in periodicals.
Most of these written pieces were anonymous;

but some of them came avowedly from men of recognized eminence in various fields of intellectual activity.

It is with no intention of conveying the slightest suggestion of disparagement of the authors of these various articles that I say that not one of them contained a single argument which every person who has paid even a superficial attention to the history of English orthography has not been familiar with from the time of his first entering upon the study. Even the jokes and sarcastic remarks of the newspapers were hoary with the rime of age. In the case of these latter something must be conceded to the inherent difficulty of the attack, without imputing the feebleness of it, or the lack of originality in it, to mere barrenness of brain. From the very nature of things it is hard to be jocose upon a subject of which one knows nothing at all. A difficulty of a like nature attended the production of the arguments which were put forth seriously. They brought forward no new ideas; they simply inspired recollections. It is only the fact that the writers of the more elaborate articles seemed to regard the reasons they advanced as novel, if not startling, contributions to thought, which to the mind of the veteran of orthographical wars imparted a certain languid interest to what they said. One comes, in truth, to feel a sort of respect for the continuous incapacity to comprehend the exact nature of the problem presented, which year after year of discussion does not impair, nor affluence of argument disturb.

As in a number of the pieces I was privileged to see I found my own name mentioned, I trust it will not be deemed a mark of offensive egotism —egotism of one sort it assuredly is—if I take the occasion of its appearance in these articles to state my views exactly on various points connected with the subject instead of having them stated for me inexactly by others. As confessions seem now to be the literary fashion, it has seemed best to put what I have to say in that form. The method of personal statement enables me also to bring out more distinctly not merely the views held by many, but also the reasons by which their course has been influenced. This consequently may serve as an excuse for a mode of utterance which in the case of one so obscure as myself would be otherwise out of place. Still, while the sentiments indicated may be entertained by numbers, they are here to be considered as nothing more than my own individual opinions. I do not pretend to speak with authority for any person but myself, least of all for any organization which has started out to carry on the work of spelling reform. Some, indeed, of the particular views I express may possibly, or, it may be, will probably, meet with the dissent of those who hold in general the same beliefs.

Now that the storm and stress which followed the President's order is over, now that every one seems to have regained his equanimity, a fitting moment has apparently arrived to consider the whole subject itself without reference to the particular proposals of anybody or of any organization. This can be done at present with a certain detachment from the feelings which attended the heated controversy that then prevailed—at least, with as much detachment as is consistent with the possession of personal convictions. As this treatise, however, is avowedly egotistical, I may be permitted, before entering into the general discussion, to refer to a specific charge which has been regularly brought against me as well as against others. It is all the more desirable to do so because the consideration of it leads directly to the comprehension of what is really the great mainstay of the existing orthography. The charge is that in what I publish I do not use myself the new spellings, save, at least, on the most limited scale. I am inconsistent. My practice does not conform to my pretended belief.

Now it is very easy to retort the charge of inconsistency. No one can use our present spelling without being inconsistent; for English orthography is nothing but a mass of inconsistencies. Take one of the commonest of illustrations furnished by those opposed to any reform. You must not drop the *u* from *honour*, they tell us, because that unnecessary vowel shows that the word was derived immediately from the French, and only remotely from the Latin. On the contrary, you must retain the *b* of *debt* and *doubt*, though this letter hides their derivation from the French *dette* and *doute*, and gives the erroneous impression that they were taken directly from the Latin. Still, it is no real justification for one's own conduct to prove that similar conduct is pursued by those who criticise him for it. Let me bring forward a few reasons which have influenced my own action, as doubtless they have more or less that of others.

There is, first, the printing-office to be consulted. This has generally an orthography of its own, and does not like to have it deviated from. There is next the publisher to be considered. Even if he is personally indifferent on

5

the subject of spelling, he has a pecuniary interest in the work he is bringing out. Naturally he is reluctant to have introduced into it anything which will tend to retard its success with the public. As he usually has the means of enforcing his views, he is very much inclined to employ them.

But far more important, far more restraining than the attitude either of printer or publisher is that of the public itself. It is not simply indifferent: it is largely hostile. To many men a strange spelling is offensive; by the ill-informed it is regarded as portending ruin to the language. Necessarily no writer desires to limit his possible audience by running counter to its feelings in a matter which has no direct bearing upon the subject of which he treats. In my own case the public—most unwisely, as it naturally strikes me—is none too anxious under any circumstances to read what I write. Why, therefore, should I convert what is in my eyes a culpable lack of interest into absolute indifference or active hostility by rousing the prejudices of readers in consequence of insisting upon a point which has only a remote concern with the actual topic that may be under consideration?

These are reasons which I could fairly and

honestly give. But, after all, the main one is something entirely different, something altogether independent of the feelings of others. With advancing years knowledge may or may not come; but altruism distinctly lingers. As we get along in life most of us lose the inclination to be constantly engaged in fighting strenuously for the progress of even the most praiseworthy causes. The desire wanes of benefiting your fellow-man, while encountering in so doing not merely his indifference, but his active hostility; of urging him to show himself rational while his proclivities are violently asinine. Even the far keener enjoyment of rendering him miserable by making evident to his reluctant but slowly dawning intelligence how much of an ignoramus, not to say idiot, he has shown himself in his acts and utterances—even this most poignant of pleasures loses its relish if indulgence in it can be secured only at the cost of much personal trouble. This is just as true of spelling reform as of any other movement. In fact, indifference to the propagation of the truth about it may be regarded as a species of that very altruism of which I have just disclaimed the practice. If a man seriously believes that it is essential to the purity and perfection of the English language that *honor* should be spelled

7

with a *u* and *horror* without it; that *honorable* should be spelled with a *u* and *honorary* without it; that *meter* should have its final syllable in *re* and *diameter* and *hexameter* in *er;* that *deign* should terminate in *eign* and its allied compound form *disdain* in *ain;* that *convey* should end in *ey* and *inveigh* in *eigh;* that *precede* should end in *ede* and *proceed* in *eed;* that *fancy* should begin with *f* and *phantom* with *ph;* that *deceit* should be written without *p* and *receipt* with it; if, in fine, spelling in different ways words which have the same origin brings him pleasure, why not leave him in the undisturbed enjoyment of this mild form of imbecility? He will not be made happier by being made wiser.

It is natural, therefore, that the position of the man who has got along in years should tend to be rather that of a looker-on than of a participant in the strife. He feels more and more disposed to content himself with approving and applauding the work of the younger and better soldiers. My own attitude is, indeed, very much the same as that once described to me as his by my dear and honored friend, the late Professor Child of Harvard. He sometimes did and sometimes did not employ in his correspondence the reformed spellings which were recommended by the English and American philological societies.

It may be added, in passing, that these changes, with the weight of the greatest scholars of both countries behind them, were in general treated with almost absolute indifference; or, if considered at all, met usually with the same unintelligent opposition as have the lists put forth by the Simplified Spelling Board. "If I am writing," said Professor Child, "to one of these educated ignoramuses who think there is something sacred about the present orthography, I always take care to use the altered forms; but when writing to a man who really knows something about the subject, I am apt not to take the extra trouble required to conform to the recommendations made by the two philological societies."[1]

In not following my faith by my practice, I

[1] As this opinion of Professor Child has been questioned, I give here an extract from a letter written by him for publication, and printed in the *Home Journal* of New York for June 21, 1882. This paper was then engaged in gathering the opinions of scholars and men of letters on the subject of English orthography. "One of the most useful things just now," wrote Professor Child, "is to break down the respect which a great, foolish public has for the established spelling. Some have a religious awe, and some have an earth-born passion for it. At present I don't much care how anybody spells, so he spell different from what is established. Any particular individual spelling is likely to be more rational than the ordinary."

9

am perfectly willing to concede that my course is not merely inconsistent, but unmanly. I shall not quarrel with any one who calls it pusillanimous, and even mean. Intimations to that effect have been made to me more than once in private letters. These reproaches I recognize as deserved, and I therefore receive them with meekness. But one of the reasons given above for my action, or rather inaction— the hostility of readers to new spellings—points directly to the one mighty obstacle which stands in the way of reforming our orthography. It is, in truth, all-potent. Singularly enough, however, it is so far from receiving consideration that it hardly ever receives much more than mere mention.

The regard for our present orthography is not based at all upon knowledge, or upon reason. It owes its existence and its strength almost entirely to sentiment. We give it other names, indeed. We describe the motives which animate us in big phrases. We talk of our devotion to the language of our fathers, while displaying the amplest possible ignorance of what that language was. We please ourselves with the notion that in denouncing any change we are nobly maintaining the historic continuity of the speech. As a matter of fact, we are governed by the cheap but all-powerful sentiment of association. We like the present orthography because we are used to it. When once the point of intimate familiarity with the form of a word has been reached, it makes thenceforward no difference to us how wide is the divergence between the pronunciation and the spelling which is ostensibly designed to represent the pronunciation. As little difference does it make if the form with which we have become familiar not merely fails to indicate the origin of the word, but on the contrary suggests and even imposes upon the mind a belief in an utterly false derivation. Such considerations do not affect us in the slightest. We simply like the spelling to which we are accustomed; we dislike the spelling to which we are not accustomed. No one who familiarizes himself with the articles in newspapers and magazines written by the defenders of the present orthography can entertain the slightest doubt on this point. The arguments advanced amount to nothing more than this, that any new spelling employed is distasteful to the writer because it breaks up old associations.

Because hostility to change springs not from knowledge, not from reason, but almost entirely from sentiment, it must not be inferred that the obstacle it presents to reform is a slight one. On the contrary, it is peculiarly formidable. So far from being a feeble barrier to overcome, it is of the very strongest, if not the very strongest. The fact that in numerous instances it is based upon foundations demonstrably irrational does not in the least impair its influence. In any matter of controversy we can fight with assurance of success against beliefs which the holder has honestly, even if mistakenly, adopted, because he deems them to be in accordance with reason. Appeal can then be made to his intelligence. But not so in the case of a belief based primarily upon sentiment. This is constantly exemplified in controversies about politics or religion. But nowhere is the fact more conspicuous than in the matter of English orthography. To spell differently from what we have been trained to spell irritates many of us almost beyond the point of endurance. We can manage to put up with variations from the present orthography prevailing in past centuries when we come to learn enough about the subject to be aware that such variations existed. The writers of those times had not reached that exalted plane of perfect propriety on which it is our good fortune to live and move. But no contemporary must venture to free himself from the cast-iron shackles in which we have inclosed the form of our words without subjecting his action to our indignant protest.

It is vain to deny the strength of the feeling of association. Even to those who have ascended out of the atmosphere of serene ignorance in which it flourishes most luxuriantly, a new spelling is always apt to come with something of a sense of shock. No matter how fully we recognize the impropriety and even absurdity of the old form, none the less does the sentiment of association cling to it and affect our attitude toward it. As this treatise sets out to deal somewhat with my own impressions, I may be pardoned the employment of a personal exemplification of the point under discussion. German is, for practical purposes, mainly a phonetic tongue. In modern times anomalies which once existed have been largely swept away. It is merely a question of a few years when they will all go; for, Germany being a nation of scholars, scholars have there some influence. In studying the language as a boy I learned some spellings now rarely used. For instance, *thun* and *todt* appeared then in the forms here given. Now I see the one without the *h*, the other without the *d*. I recognize the propriety of the action taken in dropping the

13

unpronounced letters. But, while my judgment is perfectly convinced of its correctness, for the life of me I cannot get over a certain sense of strangeness when I come across the words in their new form—at least, it was some time before I could.

How much, indeed, we are all affected by this influence of association one illustration will make convincingly clear. In the sixteenth century there existed an occasional tendency to spell *hot* with an initial *w*. It was an effort to represent the pronunciation of the word which had begun to prevail in certain quarters. It did not drive out the present form, but it existed alongside of it. It was a spelling to which Spenser was particularly addicted. There are many instances of the use of it in the *Faerie Queene*, of which the following may serve as examples:

To pluck it out with pincers firie whot.
—*Book I, canto x, st.* 26.
He soone approached, panting, breathlesse, whot.
—*Book II, canto iv, st.* 37.
Upon a mightie furnace, burning whote.
—*Ib., canto ix, st.* 29.

Now, at the present day, anybody would be either amused at the appearance of such a form as *whot* if one so spelled the word ignorantly, or outraged if he did it purposely. But all of us in the case of *whole* are doing precisely the very thing we should condemn in the case of *whot*. In the former of these words the initial letter has now no more excuse for its existence than in the latter. *Whole*, by derivation, is precisely the same word as *hale*. The only real difference between these forms is the difference of vowel sound caused by dialectical variation. They are both related to *heal* and *health*. The closeness of the tie between them all is brought out distinctly in the phrase "whole and sound." For centuries, too, the word had the spelling *hole*. At a later period, like *hot*, it took unto itself an initial *w;* unlike *hot*, it continued to retain it. Consequently, we find exemplified in the two words the same old influence of which we have been speaking. The very persons who would be horrified, and properly horrified, at giving to *hot* the spelling *whot*, would be equally horrified at taking away from *whole* a letter which, besides being never heard in pronunciation, disguises the derivation; and the recognition of this latter at a glance is insisted upon by many as essential to the proper representation of the word as well as to their own personal happiness. Here, as elsewhere, it is sentiment that rules us, not sense.

It is unquestionably a distinct objection to the introduction of new spellings that they have the temporary effect of breaking up old associations. They consequently distract the attention of the reader from the idea the word conveys to the word itself. This would to some extent be true, even were he strongly in favor of the changes made. Necessarily this is much more the case when he is bitterly opposed to them, and honestly, no matter how unintelligently, fancies that the fate of the language is bound up with the continuance of some particular method of spelling. It is true that the frequent occurrence of a new form on the printed page soon dispels the sense of strangeness with which it is greeted at first. But to produce that effort speedily, the reader must have an open mind. An open mind, however, is just what the ordinary believer in the present orthography lacks. He not only conceives an intense prejudice against the new form itself, but he is sometimes unwilling to read the book or article containing it. This, I have already intimated, is my main reason for not adopting in practice several spellings which in theory I approve. Some of the old ones to which many are devoted are too much for even the large charity I entertain for the most un-

desirable citizens of the orthographic common-
wealth. But with others I put up because it is
only by using them that one can succeed in
getting a hearing from those who most need to
be made conscious of the extent of their linguistic ignorance and the depth of their orthographic depravity. It is the unbelievers
that require conversion, and not those who are
already firm in the faith. Accordingly, for the
sake of a temporary communication between
the multitude which still continues to sit in
linguistic darkness and him who seeks to enlighten them, the old spelling may be properly
used as a sort of material bridge over which to
trundle orthographic truth.

Necessarily, violent hostility to new spellings
has always to be reckoned with. It is by no
means so intense or so wide-spread as it was
once. The language employed is now much
more guarded. Men have come to gain some
comprehension of the boundlessness of their
ignorance of the subject, and have learned in
consequence the wisdom of putting restraint
upon expression. Intemperate invectives will,
indeed, continue to be heard for a long while yet.
Rarely, however, will they proceed from any
quarter where we have a right to expect real
intelligence. Doubtless belated survivals of the

previous era of good old-fashioned gentlemanly
ignorance will occasionally thrust themselves
upon the attention; but these ebullitions now
surprise and amuse rather than irritate. A
case in point comes to my mind. In the latter
part of 1906 I chanced to be in London during
the period when a violent controversy was going
on between the *Times* and the publishers as to
the prices at which books were to be offered
for sale. Every morning the columns of the
great daily were filled with letters on one side
or the other of the matter at issue. Naturally
the participators in this bibliopolic tournament
did not invariably confine themselves to the
special subject under discussion. Toward the
very close of the year a particularly precious
effusion on a side issue came from one of the
correspondents.[1] His patriotic soul had been
stirred to the depths by the fact, as he asserted,
that English publishers had been guilty of using
what he called American spelling in their books.
They had indulged in this heinous crime from
the ignoble lust of gain. He had declined, in
consequence, to buy works he needed and desired because they were printed in this fashion.
"It is a treason against our language and

---

[1] *Times*, December 27, 1906.

country," he wrote, "and not merely an offence against taste." Further, the writer of this extraordinary communication incidentally took pains to inform us that he had been the winner of a prize essay at Cambridge University. Presumably, therefore, he had reached an appreciable degree of mental development and was in possession of some intelligence, however little his utterances might seem to indicate it.

English scholarship has been too commonly distinct from scholarship in English; but in these latter days it creates some little surprise to find displayed publicly by a presumably educated man so gross a manifestation of all-pervading ignorance as is exemplified in the communication just mentioned. Undoubtedly there are still many who think just such thoughts, if it be proper to dignify sentiments of this sort with the name of thoughts. But it is really too late to give them public utterance—at least, with the writer's name attached. That should be safely sheltered behind the bulwark of type. Better still, such opinions should be reserved for the circle of one's private friends, either ignorant enough to sympathize with them, or too much attached to the speaker to expose them to the comment of a more intelligent, but also more unfeeling, world. Things, indeed, can-

19

not be said now that could be said with impunity, and to some extent with applause, fifty
years ago—and even twenty-five years ago could
be said with safety. During the last half century men have been running to and fro, and
knowledge has been increased. This is true in
particular of the knowledge of English orthography, of its history and its character. So
generally, indeed, have special students, and even
occasionally highly educated men, become familiar with the fact of the differences between the
spelling of the present and that of the past,
and to a less extent, with the changes that
have taken place at various periods and with
the causes that have brought them about,
that it startles one at first to discover that there
are quarters into which not even a ray of this
light has penetrated.

It is, however, no difficult matter to point
out the grand source of erroneous beliefs of this
sort. It all goes back to the sentiment of association. Unhappily this sentiment of association never receives check or correction, because
we familiarize ourselves with the language of
the past in the spelling of the present. In the
matter of orthography, the dead author is considered to have no rights which the living publisher is bound to respect. His spelling is reg-

ularly altered so as to conform to that of the particular dictionary which has been adopted in the printing-house as a sort of official guide. This is done even when the writer himself has felt and expressed solicitude as to the form in which his words should appear. There was a period when a somewhat similar treatment was meted out to his grammar. The great works of the past underwent at one time more or less revision at the hands of the veriest literary hacks, who made changes in the language in order to reconcile it to their notions of propriety of usage. Idioms had their structure sometimes modified, sometimes improved out of existence. Sentences were recast in order to correct supposed errors, and bring them into accord with the rules laid down in the latest school grammar. This was particularly true of the latter half of the eighteenth century and the beginning of the nineteenth. Hence, editions of the classic authors of our tongue then appearing can frequently not be consulted with confidence by him to whom it is of importance to ascertain, in any given case, the words, forms, and constructions actually used by the writer.

This condition of things is no longer true of the grammar and expression. Modern editors, as a general rule, pay scrupulous heed to the exact reproduction of the words and constructions of the original, whether these accord or not with their ideas of propriety. But as yet there is little of this sensitiveness of feeling about the orthography. It may be conceded that the matter is not in itself so important for a certain class of readers. The expression, after all, is the vital concern. Accordingly, in a work designed for the use of the great body of men, it may not be desirable to reproduce peculiarities of orthography so numerous and so variant from present use as to interfere with ease of reading, or distract attention from the thought to the form of the words in which the thought is clothed. While, therefore, the reproduction of the exact spelling of a classic work is essential to the educated man who desires to be acquainted with the history of the speech, it is of but subsidiary importance to perhaps a majority of ordinary readers. Even an author so late as Shakespeare would hardly have been the popular writer he is had the mass of men been compelled to read him in the spelling in which his works originally appeared. Something has undoubtedly been lost by conforming his orthography to that of the present time, but doubtless much more has been gained in the wider reading his works have received in consequence.

Considerations of this sort do not apply to works designed strictly for the specialist and the highly educated. But even in the case of the great mass of men they do not apply to works which have been published since English orthography fell under the sway of the printing-house. The variations from the existing forms are indeed increasingly numerous the farther we go back; but even where they most prevail they are not really large in number or serious in character. Certainly they would not present to an intelligent human being the slightest obstacle to ease of reading or of comprehension. Hence, we have a right to demand that the few variations which exist should be reproduced both in their integrity and their entirety; that an edition of an author belonging to these later periods should represent his spelling as well as his grammar. In the vast majority of instances—excluding avowed reprints—-this is not now the case. In the matter of orthography, rarely do editors or publishers have any conscience. The works of the past, even of the immediate past, are presented to us not in the spelling of the past, but in that of the present.

Hence, there is no occasion for surprise that such pitiful exhibitions of ignorance are so

23

constantly displayed by men from whom we
should naturally expect better things. The
large majority of even cultivated readers do not
see the words used by any great author of the
past in the way in which he himself spelled
them. They see them only as the modern
printer chooses to spell them for him. It is,
therefore, not surprising that the existing orthography should come to seem to such men not
the comparatively late creation it is, but as
something which has about it all the flavor of
antiquity. As an inevitable result, there has
been further imparted to it the odor of sanctity.
Ignorance is recognized everywhere as a mother
of devotion. Nowhere has there been a more
striking manifestation of this truth than in
the case of our spelling. The adoring worship
of it seems to be more widely diffused in England than in America—at least, it is there
more shameless in the exhibition of its lack of
knowledge, though that is saying a good deal.
We have all of late been made familiar with the
somewhat unfortunate remark of an English
writer, that the spelling of Shakespeare was
good enough for him. Now an assertion of this
sort would be worthless as an argument, even
were it based upon a foundation of ascertained
fact. We do not deprive ourselves of existing

24

facilities of any sort, because they were not only
unused, but were unheard of in the time of Queen
Elizabeth.   No one now feels himself under the
necessity of refraining from making a rapid trip
to Stratford by rail because Shakespeare was
compelled to journey thither slowly and labor-
iously over the wretchedest of roads.

But in this instance an argument, worthless
in itself, is made even more worthless, if possible,
because the facts upon which it is presumed to
be founded do not exist.   Shakespeare flourished
in a period when no eager desire existed for the
maintenance of any strict orthographic monopoly.
Within certain well-defined limits every one
spelled pretty much as he pleased.   Hence, the
same word cannot infrequently be found in his
writings, and in those of his contemporaries,
with marked diversities of form.   His usage,
furthermore, differed in some cases entirely
from any known to the modern world.   But if
his printed works fairly represent his practice,
he evinced in many instances a perverse preference for what the semi-educated call American
spelling.   Let us test the truth of this last
assertion by examining the attitude he assumed
in a matter about which an orthographic controversy has been raging for centuries.   This is
the case of certain words which, according to

one method of spelling, end in *er*, according to the other, in *re*.

As regards orthography, these words naturally divide themselves into two classes. In the first of these the termination is preceded by *c*. When this is the case the words fall under the influence of a general principle regulating pronunciation—so far as general principles can be said to regulate anything in English. According to it, *c* before the vowel *e* assumes the sound of *s*. The words of this particular class which' Shakespeare uses are *acre*, *lucre*, and *massacre*. Were they made to end in *er*, they would have to come into conflict with the rule just mentioned. As a result they would mislead, as to their proper pronunciation, those who saw them for the first time. Under present conditions, they therefore cannot well undergo any change. The only way out of the difficulty would be to substitute *k* for *c*. Such a course we have taken, for instance, in the case of the word *joke*. This comes from the Latin *joc-us* with the same meaning. At its first introduction into the speech, in the latter part of the seventeenth century, it was spelled *joque* or *joc*. It finally gave up the *c* of the original and substituted for it *k*. On the other hand, in the adjective *jocose*, we retain the letter of the primitive which we have discarded in the noun.

This state of things is modern, because in Anglo-Saxon *c* had always the sound of *k*. Consequently, in *æcer*, the original of our word *acre*, there was neither difficulty nor confusion created by the employment of the letter. All this, however, was changed by the Norman Conquest. The pronunciation of *c* was in consequence affected, as it still is, by a following *e*. The result was that for a long time *k* was largely substituted in this particular word for the original letter. But in the fourteenth century the present method of spelling it came into fashion. It has remained in fashion ever since. The earlier form maintained itself for a while as of equal authority. It, indeed, died out slowly and reluctantly; but it died at last. In the collected edition of Shakespeare's plays, which appeared in 1623, *acre* was practically the only recognized spelling. The word occurs in this work just seven times. In one instance only does the older form crop up. When Hamlet tells Laertes, "Let them throw millions of acres on us," the word is spelled *akers*.[1] In a similar way Bacon in his *Advancement of Learn-*

[1] Act V, scene 1, line 269.

27

ing uses *lukar* for *lucre*.   But examples of practices such as these are exceptional.

Consideration of a like sort does not, however, apply to the words of the second class to be considered.   There are several of these now found with the ending *er* or *re* which do not appear in Shakespeare's writings.   Conspicuous among those not used by him are *fibre* or *fiber*, *miter* or *mitre*, *niter* or *nitre*, *sabre* or *saber*, *specter* or *spectre*.   But the words of this second class which actually occur are more numerous than those of the first class.   The most common ones employed by him, about which variation of usage now prevails, are *center* or *centre*, *luster* or *lustre*, *meager* or *meagre*, *meter* or *metre*, *scepter* or *sceptre*, *sepulcher* or *sepulchre*, *theater* or *theatre*.   It becomes a matter, therefore, of some interest to discover which of these forms must be chosen by the writer who professes that Shakespeare's spelling is good enough for him.   The evidence afforded by the printed page—in this case the only evidence that can be secured—is accordingly given in the following paragraph.

Take the spelling of the words just mentioned as it is found in the folio of 1623.   *Center* appears precisely twelve times in that volume.   It is never spelled with *re*.   In ten instances it has the termination *er*. Once the form *centry* is found, and once *centure*. *Meager* occurs five times. In every instance it ends in *er*. This similar statement may be made of *meter*, which is used but twice. In both these cases it has the termination *er*. *Scepter* is a word found far more frequently. It appears just thirty-five times.[1] Not once does it have the ending *re;* it is invariably *er*. The case is not essentially different with *sepulcher*. Thirteen times it occurs; eleven times with the termination *er*, twice with the termination *re*.[2] About the theater Shakespeare may be supposed to have had some knowledge. The word itself appears but six times in his plays. But even in these few instances he seems to have felt a perverse preference for the spelling in *er* over that in *re*. The former occurs just five times, the latter but once. The only consolation left for him who combines devotion to Shakespeare with devotion to the ending in *re* is found in the word spelled *lustre* or *luster*. It appears

[1] Mrs. Cowden Clarke's Concordance gives but thirty-four. She omits the instance of its occurrence which is found in I *Henry IV.*, act ii, scene 4.
[2] The form *sepulchre* is found in the folio of 1623, in *Richard II.*, act i, scene 3, and in III *Henry VI.*, act i, scene 4.

exactly thirteen times. Seven times it is spelled the former way, six times the latter.

Spellings of this sort, it may be added, are far from being limited to Shakespeare's age. They were followed by many writers much later. Modern editions, to which we are accustomed, do more, as already intimated, than hide the fact from our eyes. They actually prevent, for most of us, the possibility of discovering it. Hence, the prevalent lack of intelligence, with its consequent hardiness of assertion, not unfrequently accompanied with the feeling of distress and repulsion at any proposal for change. He whose heart is affected with sadness at the sight of the spelling *theater* for *theatre* or *center* for *centre*, and whose prophetic soul foresees disaster as the result of the general adoption of such forms, would find his grief alleviated and his fears dispelled if he could only extend his knowledge sufficiently to familiarize himself with the real practice of the past, instead of getting his notions about it from the falsifications of the present. Examine, for instance, in regard to the very usage under discussion, the first edition of Addison's *Remarks on Italy*. This work was brought out in 1705 by Tonson, the most noted publisher of the time. The same variation which prevailed earlier in the use of these

terminations still continued. But there continued also a distinct preference for *er* over *re*.
Fiber, salt-peter, and *scepter* are found as here
printed. *Theater* occurs seven times, six times
as *theater,* and once—in poetry—as *theatre.*
Amphitheater is used ten times in all. Once
its plural is spelled *amphitheatres;* in the other
nine instances it has the ending in *er.*[1] On the
other hand, *meager* and *niter,* both of which are
used once, and *sepulcher,* which appears five
times, have the termination *re.* Or, take
Gulliver's Travels, which came out more than
a score of years later. The first edition of
the work was published in 1726 in two volumes.
In it *center* is found just seven times. In
every instance it is spelled with the ending
er, not once in *re. Meager,* it may be added,
occurs twice, and in both cases as here spelled.[2]
But here again, as in most other works, modern
reprints falsify the record.

[1] Addison's *Remarks on Italy, etc.,* ed. of 1705, *fiber,*
p. 212; *salt-peter,* p. 239; *scepter,* pp. 19, 124; *theater,*
pp. 102, 155, 156, 433 (twice), 521; *theatre,* p. 50;
amphitheater, pp. 57 (twice), 127, 176, 219, 224, 302,
345, 379; *amphitheatres,* p. 225.

[2] *Travels into Several Remote Nations of the World,*
by Captain Lemuel Gulliver, London, 2 vols., 1726.
Center appears in vol. i, pp. 60, 67; vol. ii, pp. 36
(twice), 37, 43 (twice); twice *meager* appears in vol. ii,
pp. 63, 105.

In these instances it is easy enough to exaggerate the importance of the evidence furnished on this point; at least, it is so in the case of the Elizabethans. In any fair discussion of orthography, two things are to be kept in view. One is to ascertain the exact facts; the other is not to get from them erroneous impressions. Let us go back, for instance, to Shakespeare and his spelling of words with the endings *er* or *re*. It is not in the least desirable to attribute to him feelings which he never had, nor even dreamed of having. Like his contemporaries, he found two forms of these words in use. Like them, he attached no particular sanctity to either. He unquestionably felt himself at liberty to use both. All, therefore, that one can positively say in the case of these words is that if Shakespeare had any preference, it was manifestly in favor of the termination in *er*.

If it be urged that the plays published after his death do not represent either his opinion or his practice, it is fair to say in reply that a like condition of things is revealed in the minor poems. All of these appeared in his lifetime. Over the printing of some of them he may have had no oversight. For the spelling of the words found in these he cannot, therefore, be

32

held directly responsible. Still, the two most important of them—*Venus and Adonis* and *The Rape of Lucrece*—must, in going through the press, have passed under his own eye. In consequence, the spelling employed could not have failed to receive his tacit sanction at least, if even, what is more probable, he was not himself primarily responsible for it. Yet in these very two poems *scepter*[1] and *sepulcher*[2] are found so spelled in the original editions. A like statement may be made of this last word in the single instance in which it occurs in the *Sonnets*.[3] Further, the same thing may be said about his use of *center*[4] and *meter*.[5] Each appears but once, but it appears as just given. On the other hand *meager*, which is found five times in this form in the plays, has the spelling *meagre*[6] in its solitary occurrence in the poems. For neither one of these forms is Shakespeare likely to have felt any decided preference. Still, he could not have failed to see that there was no more reason for the spelling *meagre* instead of *meager* than there was for *eagre* in place of *eager*, or, to adopt the more common earlier orthography, *egre*.

[1] *The Rape of Lucrece*, l. 217. [4] *Sonnets*, cxlvi.
[2] *Venus and Adonis*, l. 622. [5] *Sonnets*, xvii.
[3] *Sonnets*, lxviii. [6] *Venus and Adonis*, l. 931.

33

Besides these words there were two others of the class considered, about which variation of usage existed or exists. Because of their single occurrence in his writing, their spelling can be regarded of importance only as indicating tendency. Othello, in his account of his life, speaks of "antres vast and deserts idle," as it is found in all modern editions. But Shakespeare has no such form as *antres*. In the first folio it is *antars;* in the quarto of 1622 it is *antrees*, indicating a difference of pronunciation. The word itself is rare at any period. Its later use, so far as it has been used at all, is due to its appearance in a favorite play of the great dramatist. No one among his contemporaries seems, so far as is now known, to have felt it desirable or incumbent to resort to its employment; though later investigations may cause it to turn up at any time. But the form in which we know it is not due to Shakespeare himself, but to his editors. There seems little reason for denying him the privilege of spelling the word in his own way. There is still another term, now not uncommon, which is found but once in his writings. But the villainous stuff which Henry IV.'s ambassador told Hotspur was digged from the bowels of the earth to destroy brave men, was not *salt - petre,* as modern

34

editions have it, but *salt - peter* in the original.[1]

These are all the disputed words of this class which are found in the poems of Shakespeare as well as in his plays, as also the number of times of their occurrence. Facts of this sort are familiar, at least in a general way, to all special students of our speech. But even from the highly educated they are hidden more or less, and in many cases hidden altogether. These see ordinarily nothing but modern editions of the greatest writers; and in modern editions modern orthography is substituted for the orthography which the authors of the past favored, or at least endured. The result is that the feeling of association which attaches to every word a particular form is never subjected to the counteracting influence which would spring from coming even into occasional contact with the earlier usage. The strength of this feeling has in consequence become abnormal. From it has further developed the singular belief of the orthographically uneducated that the present spelling is somehow bound up with the purity of the language, if not with its continued existence.

[1] I *Henry IV.*, act i., scene 3.

It is because I look upon this sentiment of association as the main bulwark of our present orthography that I have always taken the ground that it is only through a rising generation that any thorough-going reform can ever be accomplished. It is asking too much of human nature to expect a generation already risen to go a second time through the fiery ordeal of learning to spell. Individuals belonging to it will adopt proposed changes, especially those in whom conviction is reinforced by the energy of youth or of personal character. Of these there will be a regularly increasing number with the enlightenment which is sure to follow discussion of the subject. But the action of the great mass of even highly educated men will not be affected. This state of things would probably be true of the spelling of any language; but in one so defiant of all law as our own, the aversion to change would increase in proportion to the lawlessness. We are not disposed to give up what with so much toil we have acquired. Furthermore, there comes to be in the minds of many a certain fondness for the existing orthography because of its very irrationality, of its constant unfitness to fulfil its professed aim of representing pronunciation. Its uncouthness inspires them with the same sort of devotion with which the lower order of savage tribes regard their gods. The uglier they are, the more fervently they are adored.

In the case of a rising generation there are no such feelings to be encountered. The soil is virgin. No prejudices are to be overcome, no sentiments to be shocked, no customs to be changed. The reasoning powers have not been so blunted by association that the mind looks with favor upon what is defiant of reason. Furthermore, about the changed and correct forms would speedily gather the same sentiment which has caused the previous forms to be cherished by their elders. The younger generation will in time do more than look upon the new spellings as the only conceivably rational ones. They will wonder by what perversity their fathers came to tolerate the old ones in defiance of reason. If a child has been accustomed from his earliest years to use exclusively the forms *vext* and *mixt*, the spellings *vexed* and *mixed* will not only seem offensive to him when he becomes a man, but it will be difficult for him to comprehend the precise nature of the irrationality which could ever have insisted upon it as a virtue that the combination *ed* should have the sound of *t*.

A risen generation, accordingly, cannot reasonably be expected to adopt a new spelling. The most that can be asked of it is that it shall not put itself in active opposition, that it shall let the task of improving our present barbarous orthography go on unimpeded. This, however, is the very last thing it is inclined to do. The fathers have eaten sour grapes; they have no intention of keeping their children's children's teeth from being set on edge. Yet there is plainly to be recognized now the existence of a steadily increasing number of persons who are disposed to consider this whole question carefully. In the case of such men—upon whose co-operation the success of any movement must ultimately depend—it is all-essential that the changes proposed should recommend themselves by their manifest propriety or by the probability of their general acceptance. They may be unwilling to take the trouble to use these new forms in their own practice, even if convinced of their desirableness; but they will be ready to cast their influence in favor of their adoption by the members of that rising generation to whom the spelling of certain words in certain ways has not yet become almost a second nature.

The permanent success of any spelling reform, according to this view, depends upon its adop-

38

tion by a rising generation. To have it so
adopted, it must recommend itself to the risen
generation as being both desirable and feasible.
Unreasoning ignorance, intrenched behind a
rampart of prejudice, can be ignored. Not so
the honest ignorance of those whose training
naturally inclines them to favor what has been
long received, but who are not averse to consider
the question in dispute fully and fairly. In any
case the changes proposed, in order to succeed,
must follow the line of least resistance; for they
have to encounter that peculiarly formidable
of hostile forces—the unintelligent opposition
of the intelligent. The altered forms recommended for adoption must, therefore, have at
the outset some support either in present or past
usage, or they must be in accord with the operation of some law modifying orthography, which
has always been steadily, even if imperceptibly,
at work in the language.

It is because it does not conform to either of
these principles that, had I had anything to say
about it, I should have objected to the recommendation of the spelling *thru*. My reasons for
taking such ground would have had nothing to
do with the abstract propriety or impropriety
of the new form. Nor could exception be taken
to it on the score of derivation. The original

word, indeed, from which it came was *thurh*.
Later this appeared at times as *thruh*. No fault
could, therefore, be found with the alteration
beyond the dropping of the sign of the no longer
pronounced guttural. It is not principle,
therefore, that would have come into the
consideration of it, but expediency. I should
have objected to it solely on the ground that
it is a violent break with the literary past.
Therefore, instead of following the line of least
resistance, it would follow the line of greatest.
It would be sure, in consequence, to excite bitter
hostility and to repel support from the other
recommendations made. Its adoption into the
list would, therefore, not have seemed to me
good policy. This is a view of the matter entirely independent of my personal indisposition
to favor vowel changes in the spelling until a
settled plan for the representation of the vowel
sounds has been agreed upon and accepted.
Yet it is fair to add that in consequence of the
frequency with which the new form has been
made the subject of attack, the sense of strangeness and the resultant hostility with which it
was first greeted have now largely worn away.

It has been asserted that hostility to the very
idea of reforming the spelling has largely its
source in the erroneous beliefs, with the prej-

udices engendered of them, that have come to prevail in consequence of tampering with the orthography found in the works of the past, and reproducing them in the orthography of the present. In time, and with effort, the widely diffused ignorance so generated can be trusted to disappear. But even when this obstacle is removed, another of the same general nature still remains. It is, perhaps, full as formidable. There is no reference here to the difficulty inherent in the very character of our spelling— a difficulty that is far the most serious of all. This is, however, a subject which will come up for consideration by itself. The obstacle here in mind lies in the very nature of the men of our race. It is an obstruction by no means confined to them; only in them it is more pronounced than in the case of other nations with other tongues. The English-speaking people, in their attempts at carrying out any reform, are little inclined to act logically. They do not place clearly before themselves the exact nature of the evil they propose to attack, and then set out to extirpate it root and branch, according to certain well-defined principles. On the contrary, they work by the rule of thumb. They find a flaw here, a defect there. They then proceed to remedy it as best they can without disturbing and disarranging the rest of the structure. Accordingly, no symmetry is displayed in the character of the alteration made and no perfection in the result.

Still, about this method there are manifest advantages. Whatever changes are effected are effected with the least possible friction, and after the least possible struggle. They are brought about so gradually that the minds of men are comparatively little disturbed by the break with the past which has been made. There still remain relics of its absurdities with which they can console themselves for what they have lost. Consequently, the alterations, however much an object of dislike, cause nothing of that intense hostility which attends any scientific and, therefore, sweeping reform.

In this respect our race stands in sharpest contrast with that foreign one with which its connections have been closest—which has often been its enemy and occasionally its ally. The French mind, unlike the English, is by nature severe and logical. It cares little for precedent. It fixes its eyes upon principle. It is disposed to follow any reform it accepts to its remotest conclusion. It drops without hesitation long-cherished excrescences, brings order out of chaos, even if in so doing it is forced to disregard traditions and override cherished sentiments. We can see the attitude of the French mind as contrasted with that of the English best illustrated in comparatively recent French history. The Revolution was a period of storm and stress. Things were then attempted which would hardly have been thought of, far less tried, at any ordinary period. But the point here is that such things could never have been carried out by the men of the English race at the most extraordinary period. It is not merely that they would not have been done; they would not have been contemplated. To unify France, for illustration, it was essential, in the eyes of the revolutionists, that the ancient provinces should be obliterated, so far as their size would permit their entire effacement. They therefore cut up the land into departments. In these the old boundaries were disregarded. Sections of different provinces were brought into political union wherever practicable. New affiliations were to take the place of the old. The idea of federation was to be destroyed. The provinces were to be made to disappear as living entities from the minds of men. In place of them the department, a purely artificial creation, was to be constantly before their eyes. Men were no longer to be

Normans or Bretons or Gascons or Burgund-
ians; they were to be simply Frenchmen. In
diverting the thought of the people from the
provinces to the whole country, the reformers
had no hesitation in uprooting the traditions
and common associations which the inhabitants
of these provinces had inherited from the past,
and in running counter to sentiments which had
been the outgrowth of centuries.

It is safe to say that in the time of most violent revolution, no idea of this sort would occur
to the men of the English-speaking races. Even
in the case of the counties of Great Britain,
where the tie is by no means strong, it can hardly be conceived as undergoing consideration.
But contemplate the reception that would be
given to the project of breaking up the United
States into a series of departments, or provinces,
in which the present boundaries should be
obliterated, and in which all the members should
have, as far as possible, the same size or the
same population! Now there would be with us
no advantage worth mentioning in any such
action. But suppose there would arise from it
advantages which every one would admit to
be of the most immense and far-reaching importance? Even in that case, imagine the favor
any such proposition would meet with, and the

chances there would be for its adoption. Yet this is something which revolutionary France not only set out to accomplish, but actually did accomplish. She accomplished it, too, not in the case of political entities which, as with us, had often only a few years of existence, and at best but two or three hundred, but in the case of provinces whose history went back to the very beginnings of modern Europe. She overrode all local ties, all provincial prejudices, in her resolution that her inhabitants should no longer be citizens of Provence or Normandy or Brittany, but citizens only of France.

Exactly the same thing may be said of another experiment then made. It is practically inconceivable to imagine the men of our race, on their own initiative, devising and setting up such a violent alteration of all existing practices as was involved in the introduction, in 1799, of the metrical system of weights and measures. There is no need of discussing here its abstract superiority or inferiority. The only point to be made prominent is that the English could not, or at least would not, have gone at the problem that way. Even if they had solved it to their satisfaction, they would not have thought of at once proceeding to put into practice the conclusions reached. The French mind, clear and logical, saw, as it believed, the advantage of a uniform system of weights and measures. One method, for illustration, of weight for gold and silver, another for drugs and chemicals, another for ordinary objects, struck them as having no justification in reason. They took advantage of a period when all ancient beliefs and customs were on trial for their life to reduce these varying practices to uniformity. They created a commission of men to study the subject. To them they intrusted the consideration of it, and instructed them to report the measures that ought to be taken. Once satisfied that their recommendations were worthy of adoption, they did not, as would have been done with us, pigeon-hole the report containing them. Instead, they enacted them into law and imposed them upon the whole country, whether men were willing to accept them or averse.

This is the way the French mind works, or, rather, is disposed to work; for the things accomplished then could not have been accomplished so suddenly, if even at all, in any ordinary period. But the English mind does not act in that way. Just as it is in the French blood to reduce everything to a system of orderly completeness, no matter what inconveniences may attend the process, so it is in our blood to love an anomaly for its own sake, frequently to extol it as something desirable in itself. This difference of mental attitude between the two races is made strikingly manifest in their treatment of this very subject of spelling. A difficulty of somewhat the same nature, though far less in degree, confronts the French as confronts the English. Their orthography is wretched. It is not by any means so wretched as ours. Still, it is bad enough to attract the attention of men of learning and of those engaged in the business of education. The evil was admitted. What should be the nature of the remedy? To what extent should, or rather could, reform of the orthography be carried? These are not revolutionary times, and things which are capable of being carried through in revolutionary times cannot even be attempted now. Therefore, one point assumed the place of prominence. This was not what it was theoretically desirable to do, but what, under modern conditions, it was practicable to do. Accordingly, as far back as 1903, the French government appointed a commission to consider the matter. It embraced some of the most eminent scholars. The committee made a report, which was submitted by the government to the French

Academy. Disagreement arose, not so much on matters of principle as of detail. A second commission was appointed to prepare a final plan upon which the minister of public instruction could take action. Its report has been published and its conclusions promulgated. They are not binding, to be sure. Yet, with the weight of the government and the French Academy behind them, it is merely a question of time when any changes recommended will be adopted by all.

It is evident from this one fact that the desire to make the spelling conform as far as possible to the pronunciation—the one object for which spelling was devised—is far from being confined to the men of the English-speaking race. Even when it cannot succeed in its main object, it aims to bring about uniformity by sweeping away the anomalous. The movement for spelling reform now going on with us is, therefore, no isolated undertaking. It is simply part of a world-wide movement in the interests of law and order. There is an intellectual conscience as well as a moral one. On this subject the intellectual conscience of the users of speech among all thoroughly enlightened nations has now been distinctly awakened. The only peculiarity about English is that the need of such an awakening is far more pressing than in other tongues, and

the difficulty of discovering the right track to
follow is far greater. Neither Italian nor Spanish requires any sweeping change. For all
practical purposes, these tongues are phonetic.
Irregularities can unquestionably be found, but
they are neither numerous nor important.
Above all, they do not affect the vital representation of pronunciation by giving, as with us,
different signs to the same sound and different
sounds to the same sign. Their deviation from
the phonetic standard is confined to the retention of unnecessary letters. This is a matter
that can be grappled with easily. On the
limited scale it exists, it is not of much moment.
Any variations from the ideal can be easily corrected if the project is once taken seriously in
hand.

In German, the variation from the phonetic
standard is greater than in the two tongues just
mentioned. As compared with English, however, it is exceedingly slight. Even in those
instances where it has different signs to represent
the same sound, it does not, as is the case with
our speech, make the confusion more confounded
by giving to these same signs the representation
of sounds altogether different. But the public
mind is awake in Germany to the importance
of this subject. Many of the more marked

variations from the phonetic ideal have already been done away with by the action of the several governments. For, in Germany, a nation of scholars, the control of educational methods is immediately or remotely in the hands of scholars. These men, not satisfied with what has already been accomplished, are at work to do away with the anomalies that continue to exist. When once they come into accord over the measures to be adopted and the changes to be made, it is merely a question of time when their proposals will be carried into effect. The various governments will do the work of promulgation and enforcement. The reforms recommended will be embodied in the text-books and taught in the schools. That action once taken, the whole work itself has practically been done.

Unfortunately, none of the means just mentioned are practicable with us. The administration of education is nowhere in England or America really centralized, as it is in France and Germany. In those countries any changes which have behind them the best expert opinion can be carried through with comparative ease. The German government will venture on any educational experiments which have the united support of German scholars. In France the almost superstitious deference paid to the

decisions of the Academy will cause any orthographic changes having the sanction of that
body to be accepted by the great mass of the
community. Individuals may growl, but they
will submit. More than once the Academy has
recommended reforms, and these have been
adopted because they were so recommended.
About the middle of the eighteenth century it
altered the spelling of five thousand words.
Perhaps it would be juster to say that it indicated, in the case of a number of these, what
one should be adopted of several forms which
were then in use. No one would think now
of going back to those against which it then
pronounced. When, therefore, the department
of public instruction and the Academy work
together in harmony, their union is irresist-
ible. Once the reformed spelling is authorized
to be taught in the public schools, the simpler
forms can be trusted to work their way by that
inherent strength of their own which comes
from inherent sense. Of course, objection will
be made; but it will manifest itself in little else
but empty spluttering or impotent invective
on the part of those who mistake custom and
association for reason, and fancy that the life
of a word is found in the form in which they
are in the habit of seeing it clothed.

"They order these matters better in France," are the words with which Sterne begins his *Sentimental Journey*. Any action of the sort just mentioned is impossible with the men of the English-speaking race. We have neither the machinery to use, nor the disposition to use it, if we had it. There is nowhere, either in England or America, any great centralized authority, literary or administrative, to which deference if not obedience is felt to be due. With us in the United States in particular, we have no national government which can authorize examination of the subject, still less enforce any action. As little respect is paid to the conclusions of scholars who have made the matter a special study. With a great body of men the words of the veriest ignoramus who is able to get access to the columns of a newspaper are as likely to be heeded as those of him who has spent years in the investigation of the character and history of English orthography. But if the ignoramus is merely an ignoramus in this subject, if he chances to be a man who has shown ability and gained deserved repute in some other distinct field of endeavor, the authority he has justly secured for himself in matters he knows a great deal about is transferred to any pronouncements he chooses to make in a matter he knows little or nothing about. In considering the construction or reconstruction of a bridge or building, every one is willing to defer to the judgment of experts. When, however, it comes to the consideration of spelling, there is no one who does not have the comfortable consciousness that on this question his opinion is distinctly more valuable than the conclusions reached by the wretched cranks who have taken pains to master the subject, and are necessarily hampered in the views they entertain by the knowledge they have been unfortunate enough to acquire.

Therefore, as contrasted with other nations and races, we are at a disadvantage. We have not the controlling influence of an academy. The government cannot well take the initiative. If one party embraced it, the other party would be fairly sure to set itself in opposition. This would not be necessarily because of any dislike to the project itself, but for the sake of making party capital. "If I were younger," once remarked Gladstone, speaking of the spelling, "I would gladly take hold of this reform." Had he done so, can any one doubt that whatever scheme he proposed would have had arrayed against it all those who were hostile to the views he advocated on other subjects, irrespective of any feelings they chanced to entertain on this particular one. Political machinery, so constantly used to effect reforms, is consequently barred. In every English-speaking country the general government cannot well take any action, except under the impulse of a popular demand too wide-spread and too powerful to be resisted. There is, furthermore, in this country a special difficulty. In America it is not the action of the general government that is of importance, but the independent action of the several states. Even if reform were carried through in some of them, there would always be danger of discordant measures being taken in others.

Only one resource, therefore, is left to the men of English-speaking countries. It is by the slow processes of discussion and agitation. The great mass of men must be convinced by methods which will convey to the general mind the truths that are known now only to the few. They must be made to see both the desirableness and the practicability of change before any wide-reaching results can be secured. They must be made to see the futility of the arguments by which men seek to bolster up the pretensions of the existing orthography; the waste of time and efforts involved in its acquisition, and even in its use. More than all—though this is a matter little touched upon—they must be made to recognize the actual mental injury wrought to the young by its present condition. The accomplishment of this is not merely a great work, but in English-speaking lands it is one peculiarly difficult. In other countries it is necessary to convince those who have more or less studied the subject; for in their hands lies largely the control of the machinery of education. But with us it is necessary to convince those who are unfamiliar with the subject, and who not unfrequently have had their ignorance strongly reinforced by prejudice. In the multitude of these is found no small proportion of the educated class.

CHAPTER II

THE unintelligent opposition of the intelligent! I have specified this as the most formidable of the active forces hostile to reform of English orthography. No duty is imposed upon those who have that end in view more arduous than that of propagating knowledge among the educated classes. It is hard to enlighten the ignorant man. But as regards this particular subject, his mind is practically a blank page. As he has not mastered the conventional spelling, he not only has no knowledge of it, but he is aware that he has no knowledge of it. But in the case of the educated man there is nothing of this open-mindedness. In his opinion he knows already everything about the subject that can be known or that is necessary to be known. It is only within a very recent period that he has begun to suspect his limitations. Only within a recent period has he exhibited any hesitation about exposing to the gaze of the public the scantiness of the intellectual wardrobe with which he is clad.

This imputation of ignorance of the subject has been much resented. Nowhere has the resentment been keener than where the ignorance is manifestly profoundest. To the fact itself not any opprobrium necessarily attaches. No educated man considers it discreditable to lack knowledge of the chemical constituents of the food he eats, or of the things he sees and handles every day. If, indeed, because of his familiarity with these objects, he fancies that he is competent to form a judgment about their properties and draws conclusions as to their use, then his course becomes objectionable. It is exactly so in language. Pronunciation, and the proper way of representing it in spelling, and the ways in which it has been represented at various periods—these are subjects which demand long and severe study before one has a right even to state facts. Naturally, still less has he a right to draw conclusions. He who presumes to sit in judgment upon the questions in controversy without having undergone this preliminary training, no matter if he possess ability, has little reason to complain if his pretensions meet with a good deal of contempt from those who have paid even a comparatively

57

slight attention to the subject. That his utterances are received with favor by a public as ignorant as himself is no evidence of his fitness to discuss the matter in dispute. It is simply proof of the existence of that wide-spread belief in the community, that because a person may have attained deserved eminence in some field of literary activity, about which he knows a great deal, he is therefore entitled to speak with authority in some other field of which he knows little or nothing.

This unintelligent hostility of the intelligent is an obstacle peculiarly difficult to overcome, because it is based upon the combination of the minimum of knowledge with the maximum of prejudice. These characteristics frequently meet, too, in those who on other disputed subjects have the right to demand respectful attention to all they choose to say. To this class belong many men of letters—not by any means all of them, and far more of them in England than in America. Some of these have made themselves conspicuous by the violence of their utterances, some by the extent of their misapprehension of the question at issue, and some by the display of a store of misinformation so vast and varied that one gets the impression that no small share of their lives must have been spent in accumulating it. To many persons it does not seem to occur that before discussing English orthography it is desirable to equip one's self with at least an elementary knowledge of its character and history. As the acquisition of this preliminary information is not deemed essential, there is little limit to the surprising statements made upon this subject and the more surprising facts by which they are fortified. The annals of fatuity will in truth be searched in vain for utterances more fatuous than some of those produced in the course of the controversy aroused by the President's order. There is a strong temptation to substantiate this assertion by illustrating it from sayings and writings of those who took a part in it opposed to spelling reform. But it is not desirable to impart to the discussion of the subject a personal character by selecting such examples from the utterances of living persons. That the statement of the ignorance of men of letters is not unwarranted, however, can be shown as well by bringing in the testimony of the dead. In this instance it will be taken from an author of the past generation, of highest literary eminence.

Many will remember an essay of Matthew Arnold on the influence of academies, that panacea for all literary and linguistic ills so constantly held before our eyes. According to him they raised the general standard of knowledge so high that no one could wantonly run counter to its requirements and escape with impunity. The force of critical opinion would control the vagaries and correct the extravagant assertions of the most learned. In the case of our own tongue he adduced an illustration of the injury wrought to the language by the lack of such a central authority. It was taken from what he told us was one of those eccentric violations of correct orthography in which men of our race wilfully indulge. The offender was the London *Times*. That paper for a good part of the nineteenth century was addicted to printing the word *diocese* as *diocess*.

This act aroused Arnold's indignation. It is clear from his words that resentment for the course of the London *Times* in this matter had long been rankling in his bosom. A lawless practice of such a sort could not have been possible, he felt, in a country where speech had been subjected to the beneficial sway of an academy. Only in a land where no restraining influence was exerted upon the performances of the educated class could such a violation of linguistic knowledge and literary good taste be permitted. Here are his words:

"So, again, with freaks in dealing with language; certainly all such freaks tend to impair the power and beauty of language; and how far more common they are with us than with the French! To take a very familiar instance. Every one has noticed the way in which the *Times* chooses to spell the word 'diocese'; it always spells it diocess, deriving it, I suppose, from *Zeus* and *census*. The *Journal des Débats* might just as well write 'diocess' instead of 'diocèse,' but imagine the *Journal des Débats* doing so! Imagine an educated Frenchman indulging himself in an orthographic antic of this sort, in the face of the grave respect with which the Academy and its dictionary invest the French language! Some people will say these are little things. They are not; they are of bad example. They tend to spread the baneful notion that there is no such thing as a high correct standard in intellectual matters; that every one may as well take his own way; they are at variance with the severe discipline necessary for all real culture; they confirm us in habits of wilfulness and eccentricity which hurt our minds and damage our credit with serious people."

No one will question the earnestness with which these words are spoken. The difficulty with them is that they are at variance with the severe discipline necessary for all real culture —the discipline which forbids us to discuss magisterially matters we know nothing about. Consequently, they are of particularly bad example because of the eminence of the writer. What are we to think of the opinions of an author who could presume to express himself in this manner on what he called correct orthography? Where did he get his knowledge of that somewhat elusive substance? How was he enabled to pronounce authoritatively on the proper spelling of a word about whose origin and history he had not taken the slightest pains to inform himself? Arnold supposed that the London *Times* may have derived *diocess* from *Zeus* and *census*. Where did he himself think it came from?

Still, as these words of his have been more than once triumphantly quoted as an unintended, and therefore all the more crushing, argument against spelling reform by a leading man of letters, it may be worth while to give a brief account of the actual facts in regard to the appearance of *diocese* in our speech, and the changes of form it underwent—so far, at least,

as dictionaries of various periods have recorded
the usage. By so doing one may gain some
conception of the amount of research necessary
to pronounce positively upon the orthographic
history of even a single word. He will further
learn to recognize the wisdom of refraining from
the expression of large judgments upon the
correctness or incorrectness of a particular
spelling which are based upon limited knowledge. To clear the ground, it is to be said—
though it seems needless to say it—that the
first part of the word *diocese* has nothing to do
with Zeus, though one gets the impression that
its genitive *Dios* was in some way associated
with it in Arnold's mind. It comes remotely
from a Greek word meaning the management
of a household. After its appearance in our
language in the fourteenth century, various were
the forms it assumed. Students of Chaucer are
well aware that his spelling of it was *diocise*.
But it occurs but once in his writings, and then
as a ryme to *gyse*, the modern *guise*. Later,
under Latin influence, and for phonetic reasons,
it became commonly either *diocesse* or *dioces*.

Between these two forms the language seems
finally to have made a sort of compromise by
recognizing the claims of both. It dropped the
e from the one or it added an *s* to the other, just

63

as one is disposed to look at it. Though there were other forms, *diocess* became accordingly the standard. Such it remained for a long period. But its triumph was slow and, comparatively speaking, late. *Diocesse* is the form given, for example, in Minsheu's *Guide to the Tongues*, which appeared in 1617. In Edward Phillips' dictionary of 1658, entitled *A New World of Words*, it is *dioces*. But in later editions—certainly in that of 1696—*diocess* is the spelling found. Such also was the form of the word in Bullokar's dictionary of 1684; in the *Glossographia Anglicana Nova* of 1719; and in Edward Cocker's English dictionary of 1724— the only editions of these works I have had the opportunity to consult. On the other hand, in Coles's English dictionary of 1713, it is *diocese*. This is repeated in the edition of 1717. It is the earliest instance I have met of the modern spelling, though others may exist.

Before the publication of the dictionary of Dr. Johnson in 1755, the two principal works of this character which the early part of the eighteenth century produced were that of Bailey, and that of Dyche improved and completed by Pardon. The former was the first to appear. It indeed seems always to have outranked in popular estimation its successor and rival. It came out first in 1721. Before the end of the century it had passed through a very large number of editions. At the outset its spelling of the word under consideration was *diocess*. So it remained in the half dozen editions that followed. But after 1730 *diocese* took its place, and held it during the whole of the eighteenth century. On the other hand, Dyche's dictionary, which began to be published in 1735, not only authorized *diocess*, but clung to it in subsequent editions. Later in the century — certainly in the seventeenth edition of 1794—it permitted the alternative spelling *diocese*. This practice, indeed, can be met much earlier. For instance, in the second edition of Benjamin Martin's dictionary, which appeared in 1754, both *diocese* and *diocess* are given.

It was the choice of *diocess* by Doctor Johnson that turned the tide for a while in one direction. For the rest of the century it settled the spelling, so far as the practice of most men was concerned. He was followed by nearly all the later lexicographers. This was true in particular of Sheridan and Walker. These two were widely accepted as authorities, especially the latter. The edition of Walker's dictionary, which came out in 1802, just after his death, but containing his latest revisions, was long regarded by our fathers as a sort of orthographic and orthoepic statute - book. It still showed *diocess* as the only way of spelling this particular word. So did the dictionary of James Sheridan Knowles, which was first published in 1835. It continued to retain this form of the word in the editions of 1845 and 1877. It is found even in the edition of Walker, as revised by Davis, which appeared in 1861. On the other hand, Smart's revision of the same work, or remodelling, as he called it, was largely responsible for the prevalence and general adoption of *diocese*. This dictionary was first published in 1836. It had a wide circulation, and for a long time its successive editions were regarded as authoritative works of reference.

This survey of the matter is by no means exhaustive, but it is sufficiently complete to render certain the results reached. It shows that a long contest went on between the two forms of the word, and that the later gradually triumphed over the earlier. It shows too that *diocess*, though slowly going out of fashion, continued still in the best of use long after Arnold had reached maturity. As always happens, indeed, there was a certain body of conservatives who refused to accept what was in their eyes the new - fangled monstrosity.

66

The ancient usage was good enough for them.
Among these the London *Times*, owing to its
position in the newspaper world, occupied a
specially prominent place. It not impossibly
felt that in standing by the time-honored
diocess it was resisting an insidious attempt to
ruin the language.

All, therefore, that Arnold needed to do, before
expressing his opinions, or rather his prejudices,
in the matter was to learn these easily accessible
facts. To use his own phraseology, it was incumbent upon him to let his mind play about
the subject until he had fully informed himself
upon it. His failure to do this led him to fall
into the mistake he did. A note to the later
edition of his essays conveys the glad tidings
that the London *Times* has at last renounced
the error of its ways, and has succumbed to the
authority of fashion. Like the rest of us, it
now spells the word *diocese*. But the irrevocable
printed page will continue to stand and bear
perpetual witness to the blunder of its critic.

One is not, indeed, astonished at the lack of
familiarity with the facts just recorded on the
part of a man of letters. They lie outside of his
particular province. They are not, indeed,
generally known. Nor are they in themselves
so exciting as to attract the attention, still less

the study, of anybody, without some external provocation. Ignorance of them is, therefore, nothing discreditable. Indeed, we may almost expect it from those who have made the study of literature their pursuit in contradistinction to that of language. It gives one, however, a sort of shock to find that this same ignorance has been occasionally exhibited by linguistic scholars of the previous generation. A kind of sanction is given to Arnold's assertion by the remark of Richard Gordon Latham on this same word *diocese*. In his revision, published in 1871, of Todd's edition of Johnson's dictionary, he observed under it that it was "once ignorantly spelled *diocess*." No wonder that the *Times* succumbed to this combined attack of learning and letters marching under a common banner of inadequate investigation and erroneous assertion.

I have gone at great length into the consideration of this particular example, not entirely from the eminence of the author who chose to furnish it. As much were these details supplied in order to make manifest how patient and protracted must be the study which will authorize any one to pronounce decisively upon a question of disputed spelling. As long as the advocates of the existing orthography confine

68

themselves merely to the expression of their
prejudices and opinions, they are comparatively
safe, even though their prejudices have no foundation in reason and their opinions have behind
them no trace of investigation. The moment,
however, they attempt to fortify their notions
by illustrations and argument, they are lost.

This is the moral of the tale told of Arnold.
There are circumstances in which no amount of
genius can make up for the lack of a little accurate knowledge. It is not often given to an
essayist to exemplify himself a practice he
vehemently condemns in the very paragraph
containing the condemnation. If academies
really exerted the power with which Arnold
credited them; if they could exercise a controlling influence over public opinion; if they
could establish so broad a basis of intelligence
that men would be prevented from giving utterance to crude and hasty dicta; if they could
keep writers from palming off upon the public
the results of imperfect knowledge acting through
the medium of perfect prejudice—if these things
were so, it is quite clear that in this particular
instance it would have been the utterances of
Matthew Arnold that would have been suppressed, and not the assumed orthographical
vagaries of the London *Times*. In Germany,

where there is no academy, but where there is a broad and lofty level of linguistic intelligence, observations of a similar character would have met with immediate and crushing exposure and censure. In England and America, where there is a broad and deep level of linguistic ignorance, this blundering statement has long been hailed by many as a proper rebuke to the miscreants who are seeking to defile the sacred altar of English orthography.

An extravagant outburst like the one just cited—it could easily be paralleled from recent utterances—coming from a man occupying a far higher position than any literary defender of the present spelling, reveals what a fathomless abyss of ignorance and prejudice must be filled up or bridged over before there can be even a calm discussion of the subject by the mass of educated men. If we are unable to treat with respect the utterances of great men who are capable of falling into errors like the one just exposed, how can we be expected to be impressed by the words of little men who cite these easily detected blunders as an authoritative justification for their own hostility? Because they deal with language as an art, they fancy they know all about it as a science. There is no intention of conveying the impression that men of letters

are more remarkable than others for erroneous
assertions on this subject. As a class they are
probably less so. In their ranks, too, are to be
found some of the most earnest sympathizers
with the movement for the simplification of
the spelling. These, too, stand in the first rank.
It must not be assumed, therefore, that those
among them who have gained an unenviable
notoriety by the blunders into which they have
fallen in opposing it are more ignorant than
other men. They have simply had furnished
them by their position unequalled opportunities
to make their ignorance conspicuous.

Now, to any real student of the subject, it is
evident that both in French and in English the
most conservative of courses has been contemplated and taken, so far as any change in
orthography has been recommended. No attempt has been made to introduce phonetic
spelling. Any intention of that sort has been
distinctly disclaimed by those among us who
have set the reform on foot. Yet it is a charge
from which they have been unable to escape.
One of the most striking as well as most entertaining features of the controversy that
went on was the persistent assertion of those
concerned in the movement, that they had no
design or desire to introduce phonetic spelling;

and the equally persistent assertion of their assailants that it was the very thing they were aiming to introduce. One side laid down precisely what it sought to do. The other side denounced it for doing the very thing it disclaimed doing. One side declared that it purposely limited its efforts to the removal of some of the anomalies in our present orthography, and the obstacles put by these in the way of its acquisition. The other employed two methods of attack: on the one hand, it inveighed against its opponents for going as far as they did; on the other, it reproached them for their inconsistency in not going further.

Any one who has the slightest conception of what a reform of our spelling on pure phonetic principles means will absolve those now urging reform from putting forward any scheme of that sort. It requires, indeed, a singular innocence of all knowledge of this particular subject to make such a charge. Certain changes recommended would, indeed, have brought particular words nearer a phonetic standard. But if everything proposed were to be universally adopted—and even ten times more—the real disease which afflicts our orthography would be but partially alleviated. It would do little more than set us on the road to a thorough-going reform. No one, indeed, who comprehends what is required, in a language so lawless as ours, to bring about a perfect accordance between orthography and orthoepy, is ever likely to underrate the difficulties which stand in the way of the establishment of phonetic spelling, even were men as eager for its adoption as they are now hostile to it. In the present state of feeling, therefore, no one need distress himself about its immediate coming.

But why should any one distress himself at all? Little is there more extraordinary to witness in these days of assumed general enlightenment than the horror which many estimable persons seem to feel at the danger of being devoured by this dreadful ogre which they call phonetic spelling. They have no idea what it is, but they know from its name that it must be something frightful. Now, written language was designed to be phonetic. Its intention, however incomplete its realization, was to represent invariably the same sound by the same letter or by the same combination of letters. This idea lies at the root of the conception of the alphabet; otherwise the alphabet would have had no reason for its existence. To picture to the eye the sound which has fallen upon the ear, so that it should never be mistaken for anything else, was the problem that presented itself to the man or men who devised that invention which, imperfect as it is, still remains the greatest and most useful to which the human mind has given birth. To represent a sound by one character in one place and by another in another would have seemed to them as absurd as it would to a painter to have the figure of a horse stand for a horse in one picture, and in another picture for a different animal. Of course, in this comparison the symbol is in one case real, and in the other arbitrary; but the underlying principle is the same.

So far as the original invention of the alphabet failed to secure the individual representation of every sound then used, the invention was itself incomplete and imperfect. So far, again, as the characters of the alphabet have been diverted from their original design of representing particular sounds, it is not an application of the invention, but a perversion of it to inferior purposes, and to purposes for which it is not really fitted. One general statement applicable to all languages can be safely made. So far as written speech deviates from the phonetic standard, it fails to fulfil the object for which it was created. It shows to what an extent the English race has wandered away in feel-

ing and opinion from the original motives
which led men to seek the representation of the
spoken word by written characters, that its
members have come to look upon the perfect
accordance of orthography and orthoepy as a
result, not merely impracticable which is a
thoroughly defensible proposition—but as something in itself undesirable, as something fraught
with ruin to the speech itself. The written word
was devised to suggest the sound of the spoken
word. Yet this ideal is more than discredited
with us; it is treated as if it were in some way
peculiarly monstrous. Yet all there is of value
in our existing orthography is due to what still
survives of the phonetic element. This is a
condition of things which will be brought out
fully when the orthographic situation comes to
be considered.

The real life of a language consists in its
sounds, not in the signs intended to represent
them. The one is the soul of speech; the other
can hardly be considered a necessary bodily
framework, for the former could and does exist
without the latter. In earlier times, when
language was learned almost exclusively by the
ear, this fact would naturally force itself upon
the attention of every reflecting man. But with
the spread of education, when acquaintance with

a tongue is acquired largely through the eye, the knowledge of the symbolic representation of sounds has come to predominate in the minds of the men of our race over the knowledge of the sounds themselves. While all of us are familiar with the one, but few are with the other. Ask any person of ordinary attainments the number of letters in the English alphabet. He will unhesitatingly answer twenty-six; though the chances are that he will be ignorant of the fact that some of the twenty-six are really supernumerary. But extend the inquiry further. Go with it to the vast body of educated men, excluding those whose pursuits require of them more or less the study of phonetics. These being excepted, ask any single person belonging to the most highly cultivated class—opponents of spelling reform to be preferred—how many are the sounds which the letters of the alphabet and their combinations are called upon to represent. Ask him how many are the sounds which he is in the habit of employing himself in his own utterance. The chances are fifty to one that he will be utterly at a loss what to reply. He has learned the symbols of things; he has not learned the things themselves.

That this should be so in the case of our own tongue is not particularly surprising. It is, perhaps, inevitable. The attention of the men of our race has been more than distracted from any consideration of the subject by the character of our orthography. Their minds have been thrown into a state of bewilderment. As a single illustration, take the representation of the sound usually termed "long *i*." This third so-called vowel of our alphabet is not really a vowel, but a diphthong. Its sound is most commonly represented by the single letter itself, seen, for instance, in such a word as *mind*. But some idea of the uncertainty and range attending its use, with the consequent perplexity to its users, can be gathered from a few selected examples. It is represented by *ai* in *aisle;* by *ay* in *aye;* by *ei* in *height;* by *ey* in *eye;* by *ie* in *lie;* by *oi* in *choir;* by *uy* in *buy;* by *y* in *try;* and by *ye* in *dye*. Or, reverse the operation, and see how many sounds the same sign can represent. Take the combination *ou*, and observe the differences of its pronunciation in the words *about, young, youth, four, fought, would,* and *cough*.

English orthography, therefore, instead of teaching the English-speaking man the knowledge and distinction of sounds, takes the speediest and most effectual means of preventing his attaining any such knowledge. It not merely fails to call his attention to it, it forces him to

77

disregard it, to look upon it as an element not properly to be considered. He does not come to forget, he has never learned to know that there is a particular value that belongs or ought to belong to any vowel or combination of vowels. When he grows up, he is naturally ready to despise what he is unable to comprehend. The educated class has with us come generally to look upon the alphabet as a mere mechanical contrivance. They have so largely lost sight of the object for which it exists, that in many cases they are almost disposed to resent the proposition that they should employ it for the purposes for which it was created. It would be thinking too meanly of human nature to believe that men would delight in this condition of things did they once come fully to appreciate it. But to that point few of them ever arrive. Accordingly, ignorance of the real evil disposes them to look with distrust upon any attempt to remedy it.

In truth, as a consequence of the confusion which exists in the written speech, the English race, as a race, has no acquaintance whatever with sounds. It has largely lost the phonetic sense. One whole important domain of knowledge, which ought to have come to it through the spelling, has entirely disappeared from recognition without their being aware of it. Examples of the prevalent lack of any conception of the distinction of sounds and of their proper representation are brought constantly to the attention of those engaged in the work of instruction. But the comments and communications which appear in the course of any controversy on spelling reform, especially those intended to be satirical, furnish the most striking illustrations of this all-prevailing, all-pervading ignorance. There is rarely furnished a more edifying spectacle than the attempt made, in some cases by men of very genuine ability, to write what they call phonetically. In every discussion there are sure to come up with unfailing regularity certain examples that indicate the density of the darkness in which the minds of men are enveloped. Several years ago a series of articles appeared in a Western periodical attacking the reform of the orthography. In one of them occurred this observation: "We are asked," said the author, "to spell *are* without the *e*, because the letter is not pronounced. Very well: then drop the *a*, for that is not pronounced either." In the same spirit the writer went on to say that fanatical advocates of change should denote the words *see* and *sea* simply by *c*—"spelling only the letter sounded."

Here was a person producing a series of articles on orthography who was so utterly unacquainted with the primary elemental facts of orthoepy as to fancy that the sound of *r* and of *c* by themselves is the same as the name we give to those letters; who did not know that the name cannot be pronounced unless a vowel precedes the *r* in one case and follows the *c* in the other. Exactly the same examples were adduced in the course of the latest controversy. It is perfectly clear that not one of those who made use of them had the slightest conception of what was essential to convey the representation of a given sound. Any arbitrary symbol, pronounced in a particular way, seemed to them all-sufficient. Their action evinced hardly higher intelligence than would have been shown by considering the word *five* as phonetically represented by the Arabic numeral 5, which in all languages conveys the same meaning, and in all languages has a different pronunciation. One characteristic there is which denotes most distinctly the infantile state of knowledge that still continues to prevail on the whole subject. By most men any bad spelling is invariably termed phonetic spelling. That is all the idea of the latter they have. The spelling of Chaucer would in their eyes be indistinguishable in character from that of Josh Billings.

More than once have advocates of spelling reform been rebuked for the arrogance manifested by them in their references to the inaccurate assertions and loose thinking which largely make up the chatter of the uninformed on this subject. On the contrary, much of this gabble seems to me to have been treated with singular leniency. Especially has this been the case when it comes from men who have shown knowledge on other subjects and ability in other directions. These have too often missed opportunities, which were fairly obtrusive, of remaining silent on this matter. But no such forbearance is due to the rank and file of the noisy intruders into a controversy they do not understand. There was a writer who gravely informed us that it is an insuperable objection to a change in our orthography, that it would make necessary a new formative period in the history of the language. For fear that the full force of this terrible indictment should be overlooked, he proceeded to put the words containing it in italics. What possible conception could exist in the mind of such an objector as to what constitutes a formative period in the history of a language? Does spelling reform introduce new words? Does it give new meanings to old ones? Does it destroy existing inflections? Does it add any to their number? Does it vary in the slightest the order of words in the sentence? Does it cause the least modification of the least important rule of syntax? A new spelling meaning a new language! Fancy a boy refusing to wash his face, on the ground that if the dirt were removed he would not be the same boy. Fancy a man objecting to putting on a new suit of clothes, on the ground that by so doing he could never be again what he was before; that the integrity of his character and the continuity of his traditions would be destroyed; that he would no longer be the same man to those who had known him and loved him. This is not a travesty of the argument which has been advanced. It is the argument itself, applied not to the dress of the body, but to that of the speech. The men who hold such opinions are really in the same grade of intellectual development as regards language, as in literature are those who fancy that beginning a line with a capital letter is the one essential thing which constitutes poetry.

But of all the educated opponents of spelling reform, I have to confess that the most entertaining to me are women. As devotion to the present orthography is a matter of sentiment and not one of reason, it is perhaps not strange that some of the most violent opponents of the present movement are to be found among the members of that sex with which appeals addressed to the feelings are peculiarly potent. It must not, however, be assumed for a moment that this characterization is meant to apply to all women. On the contrary, among them can be found not only many of the most earnest advocates of reform, but an especially large proportion of the most intelligent and clear-headed. This observation is particularly true of those of them who are connected directly or indirectly with the profession of teaching. To the hands of women, indeed, the business of the instruction of the very young is almost entirely committed. They make themselves familiar with the character of the orthography from the side of both theory and practice. They have, in consequence, forced upon their attention, as have few men, the absurdities and anomalies of our present spelling, the unnecessary and utterly irrational obstacles it puts in the path of the learner; the time and toil which must be spent, or rather wasted, in mastering rules to which the exceptions are as numerous as the examples, and in which exceptions abound to the exceptions. The intelligent among them naturally come to know whereof they speak, and to have decided opinions born of experience and observation.

But experience and observation of this sort have not been forced upon the majority of even educated women. Acquaintance with the real nature of our orthography is not, in their eyes, a matter of intrinsic importance. Accordingly, in the case of those who feel intensely on this subject and exhibit a virulent hostility toward reform of the spelling, we can observe the peculiar mental effervescence which is produced when the maximum of emotion is allowed to operate upon the minimum of knowledge. With them the question is not at all one of argument. It is entirely one of taste, as they regard taste; though occasionally there seems to be an honest even if unfounded belief that arguments have been employed. It is their sensibilities that are outraged, not their reason. I confess to liking the attitude of these opponents of spelling reform, and to receiving gratification from their extremest utterances. They are entirely free from the sham in which men indulge, of pretending to be influenced in their beliefs on this subject by logical principles. Sojourning in that upper rarefied air of sentiment in which

common-sense staggers and reason swoons, there
is an indefinable charm in the irrationality they
display in resolutely ignoring facts they find
inconvenient to consider and arguments they
disdain to comprehend.

No pleasure, indeed, can be conceived more
delightful than in listening to the discussion of
this subject by its female opponents. As this
is largely a book of personal confessions, I may
be permitted to say that I like to hear them
talk and to read what they write. They feel
about reform of the spelling as did in another
way certain of their high-born sisters who have
left behind memorials of their experiences when
the great cataclysm of the French revolution
took place. It was apparently not the scenes
of horror and massacre that shocked these scions
of noble families; not the victims carted in
tumbrils to the guillotine; not the fusillades
which swept the streets and stained the pave-
ments with the blood of those who fell fighting
for the old régime. Nor was it the question of
right or wrong, of relieving oppression, of es-
tablishing justice. Not one of these things
seems to have made a particular impression
upon their minds. What really affected them
was something altogether different. The revolution was in such bad taste. Men like Danton

and his associates did not behave in a gentle-manly way. They were not really nice. Just so—if we can compare small things with great—is the impression one gets of the attitude of many women who are hostile to the new spell-ings proposed. Such may be nearer the pro-nunciation. They may be nearer the deriva-tion or some other old thing for which nobody cares. But these new spellings are not really nice.

This devotion of woman to the fixed orthog-raphy is largely a modern sentiment. There was little of it in the past, either in theory or practice. In fact, high position and sex were once largely regarded as entitling those belong-ing to either to be exempt from orthographic trammels. Richardson represents Charlotte Grandison as describing one of her lovers as "spelling pretty well for a lord." But in this same particular several of the most noted women in the past have also been defective. There was nothing then of the superstition of the sacred-ness of the orthography which now prevails. They apparently did not deem it possible to secure the leisure to make themselves as attrac-tive as they wished to be, were they compelled to waste their time in memorizing the exact spelling of words whose forms they had the sense to see exhibited no sense. As time went on their indifference not unfrequently came to disturb those of their lords and masters who were getting to be punctilious on this point. Swift, who in one way or another was always in a state of anxiety about the English language, had frequent occasion to chasten Stella on the subject. "I drink no aile (I suppose you mean ale)," he writes to her under date of September 29, 1710. "Who are these wiggs," he asks again on October 8, "who think I am turned Tory? Do you mean Whigs?" "Pray, Stella," he says, in April of the following year, "explain those two words of yours to me, what you mean by *Villian* and *Dainger*." "Rediculous, madam?" he expostulated, on another occasion; "I suppose you mean ridiculous: let me have no more of that; it is the author of the *Atlantis*' spelling."[1] One infers from this remark that the then noted Mrs. Manley was as notorious for the scandalous form in which her words appeared in her manuscript as she was for the scandalous meaning they conveyed when appearing in print.

One could fill page after page with the extraordinary views on spelling reform which

---

[1] Swift. *Journal to Stella*, December 14, 1710.

have come from men and women of education
and sometimes of genuine ability. The controversy, indeed, which has been going on of
late has brought out more sharply than ever
before the existence of the singular situation
which prevails in regard to it. The highly
trained expert opinion is practically all on one
side; the large preponderance of educated lay
opinion is apparently on the other. Several
eminent men have taken part in the discussion in
opposition to change. But in all their ranks
cannot be found a single one who would be recognized by special students of English as entitled to speak with authority. Not a single one
of the latter class has come forward in opposition.
Some of them are very possibly indifferent; but
so far as they have spoken—and many have
spoken—they have pronounced in its favor. If
there is among them one who entertains hostility, he is sufficiently in awe of his professional
brethren to deem it wise to keep his opinion
to the sanctity of private intercourse. No
applause of the multitude could make up to
him for the condemnation that would be his
from his peers. By ranging himself among the
opponents of spelling reform he would be well
aware that he would distinctly lose caste. He
would be placed in a dilemma on one of whose

two horns he would be impaled. He would be looked upon as guilty either of lack of knowledge or of lack of judgment.

This is a state of things that could not well exist in the case of any other subject than language. Nor, indeed, could it well happen with any other race than the English, where on both sides of the Atlantic ignorance of our tongue and of its history has been sedulously cultivated for centuries. Accordingly, the raggedest of penny-a-liners or the callowest of story-tellers considers himself as much entitled to speak with authority on the subject as he who has devoted years of study to its consideration. Of course, this is a state of things that cannot continue permanently. In the long run the opinions of the few who know will triumph over the clamors of the many who do not know. Indeed, a distinct advance has already been achieved. The subject is no longer treated with indifference. It calls forth hostile criticism, ridicule, vituperation. Furthermore, certain things can no more be said which were once said with smug satisfaction. We are now a long way beyond that provincial faith in Worcester which permitted, fifty years ago, so eminent a man of letters as Oliver Wendell Holmes to remark that Boston had for one of its distinctions "its cor-

rect habit of spelling the English language."
In these days an author of his high grade would
be saved by his inevitable association with English scholars from perpetrating an observation
so singularly crude.   Views of such a sort now
find their home only in the congenial clime of
the remote rural districts.   For slow as has been
the progress in this matter, it has been steady.
In the immediate future it is destined to advance at a much more rapid rate.   The leading
universities of America are regularly sending
out a small body of trained special students of
our speech.   In the face of this steadily increasing number of experts whose opinions are
based upon adequate investigation and full
knowledge, sciolists will in time conclude for
their own safety to learn a little before they talk
much.

Yet, neither now nor in the past has the
advocacy of spelling reform been confined to
the specialists in English study.   It has embraced scholars of all lands who paid attention
to our language or to some form of its literature.
Long ago Grimm pointed out that the greatest
obstacle to the predominating influence of the
English tongue was the character of its orthography.   But without going so far back, let
us select as types of advocates of reform three

representative men of the generation which has just passed away. They are Professor Max Müller, of Oxford; Professor Child, of Harvard; and Professor Whitney, of Yale. Of course, these scholars were cranks—"crazy cranks," if you will. Much learning had made them mad—insanity from that cause being something from which the critics of their orthographical views feel the sense of absolute immunity. Of course, we know further that professors are a simple, guileless folk, constantly imposed upon by arguments whose speciousness is at once seen by the clearer vision of the men engaged in the struggle and turmoil of practical life. To them unhappily has never been given the easy omniscience which is enabled to understand the whole of a subject without mastering a single one of its details. Still, as a member of this unpractical fraternity, and sharing in its intellectual limitations, I cannot get over the impression that there are difficulties connected with English orthography which even the very youngest newspaper writer cannot settle summarily, and questions which he cannot answer satisfactorily offhand.

In truth, the real nature of our spelling and the real difficulties connected with its reformation are not in the least understood by the vast majority of the educated class. Otherwise it would be impossible for men, sometimes of genuine ability, to give public utterance to the views they entertain. One has only to read articles in magazines and communications sent to the newspapers to gain a view both vivid and depressing of the wide-spread ignorance that prevails. It is manifest, indeed, that the nature of these difficulties is not always understood, even by those who are earnest in their desire for reform of some kind. Accordingly, before the subject can be discussed intelligently, some knowledge of the general orthographic situation must be secured. The irrepressible conflict that goes on in our speech between spelling and pronunciation can never be really appreciated, save by him who has mastered a portion at least of the details in which that conflict has reached its highest degree of intensity.

To set these details forth is anything but an agreeable task. The subject of sounds and the methods taken to represent them cannot, by the wildest stretch of the imagination, be termed exhilarating. But some notion of it must be gained by him who seeks to get any conception of what must be deemed the main trouble affecting English orthography. This is the reason, and to some must be the excuse, for presenting the results of a piece of drudgery as wearisome as it is thankless. The dose I shall try to make as palatable as possible; but there is no disguising the fact that it is a dose. But it is only by swallowing it, or something akin to it, that men can get any conception of the real evils that afflict English spelling, and of the methods that must be taken to palliate them; for in the present state of public opinion, it is hopeless to attempt to cure them. To a consideration of the orthographic situation the next chapter will therefore be devoted.

CHAPTER III

THE ORTHOGRAPHIC SITUATION

I

THE PROBLEM

IT is with a good deal of hesitation that I approach this part of my subject. To treat it fully, to consider it in all its details, would require a familiarity with the history of sounds, with their precise values, and with the proper way of representing these values, to which I can lay no claim. Though I have given some time to the study of this branch of the general question, I am well aware that my knowledge of it is not the knowledge of a professional, but of an amateur. It is only when I read the attempts of the assailants of spelling reform to write what they are pleased to call phonetically, that my own slender acquaintance with this field of research looms up momentarily before my eyes as endowed with colossal proportions. Fortunately, intimate familiarity with this par-

94

ticular part of the subject is not needed for the end had here in view. To point out the evils afflicting our present system is possible for him who is unable to prescribe a remedy. This is the special task which I set before myself in this section.

It is essential, in the first place, to have clearly before our minds the nature of the problem with which we are called upon to deal. The general statement about it may be and often is summarized in a few words. We are told that in English the same sound is represented by half a dozen signs, and the same sign is used to denote half a dozen sounds. This is all true. Unfortunately, to the vast majority of men it conveys no definite idea. It certainly would not bring clearly before them much conception of the real difficulty. Some of them would even be puzzled to explain what is meant here by the word *sign*. Most of them have no knowledge whatever of the number and quality of the sounds they use. This remark is not intended as a reproach. Their condition of ignorance is due to no fault of their own. The existing orthography does not content itself with hiding from the ordinary eye all knowledge of phonetic law; it puts a stumbling-block in the way of its acquisition. Accordingly, it does more than per-

95

mit ignorance of the subject; it fosters it. Men are not led to consider even the most aggressively prominent facts of their own utterance. I have known intelligent young persons, of much more than ordinary ability, who had never learned as a matter of knowledge that the digraph *th* has two distinct sounds; that were *thin* pronounced as is *then*, or *then* as is *thin*, we should have in each case another word than the one we actually possess. They had never confused the two in their usage, but as little had they been in the habit of remarking the difference between them. Consequently, when it was brought directly to their attention, it came upon them as a sort of surprise. If a distinction which lies on the very surface could so easily escape notice, what hope can be entertained of gaining a realizing sense of those subtler ones which abound on every side?

The first point, therefore, to be made emphatic is that there is a large number of sounds in the speech and but a limited number of signs in the alphabet. The number of sounds has been variously estimated. It depends a good deal upon the extent to which the orthoepic investigator is disposed to recognize differences more or less subtle and the weight he assigns to each. In general, it may be said that usually the lowest number given is thirty-eight, and the highest forty-four. A very common estimate puts them at forty-two. Exactness on this point is not necessary for the purpose here aimed at, and for the sake of convenience the whole number of sounds will be temporarily assumed to be forty, more or less. To represent these forty sounds we have nominally twenty-six letters. Really we have but twenty-three. Either *c* or *k* is supernumerary, as are also *x* and *q*.

Here, then, lies the initial difficulty. The Roman alphabet we have adopted has not a sufficient number of letters to do the duty required of it. For us its inability has been further aggravated by the loss of two signs which the language had originally, or acquired early in its history. For the disappearance of these there was later in another quarter a partial compensation in the differentiation of *i* and *j*, and of *u* and *v*. Of the two vanished signs one was a Rune, called "thorn" or the "thorn letter," þ, the other a crossed *d*, represented by ð. They were or could be used to represent the surd or hard initial sound heard in *thin* just mentioned, and the corresponding sonant or soft sound heard in *then*. These two letters, unknown to the Roman alphabet, were allowed to die out

of general use in the fifteenth century. Of both
the digraph *th* took the place. Yet in one way
the so-called thorn letter has left behind a
memorial of itself. Its form had something of
a resemblance to the black-letter character *y*.
Consequently, when "thorn" ceased to be used,
y was at times substituted for it. Especially
was this true in the case of the words *the* and
that. These were frequently printed as *y*ᵉ and
*y*ᵗ. This form of the latter word disappeared
after a while, not merely from use, but practically from remembrance. *Ye*, however, in
the sense of *the*, but with its initial letter given
the sound of *y*, is fondly cherished and sometimes
employed by certain persons, who indulge in
the delusion that by so doing they are writing
and talking Old English.

The use of this one digraph to represent these
two distinct sounds inevitably tends to create
uncertainty of pronunciation, if not to produce
confusion. We can see this fact exemplified in
the case of such words as *tithe* and *path* and *oath*
and *mouth*. In these *th* has in the singular the
surd sound, in the plural the sonant. The proper
way of pronouncing them has therefore to be
learned carefully in each individual instance,
for there is nothing in the spelling to indicate
it. Usage in truth is very fluctuating with re-

spect to some of the words in which this digraph appears. In consequence, the question of
their pronunciation begets at times much controversy. Still, compared with the uncertainty
attending other signs, the perplexities caused
by this are of slight importance.

The lack of a sufficient number of signs to
indicate the sounds is therefore the first difficulty to be encountered. But this is a defect
which English shares with several tongues
which have adopted the Roman alphabet.
There is another characteristic which belongs
to our language exclusively. This is the pro-
gressive movement which has gone on in the
case of some of the vowel-sounds. In the historic development of English pronunciation
several of these have lost their original values.
This has caused them not merely to deviate
from the sounds they once had in our own
speech, but has also brought them out of harmony with those of the cultivated tongues of
modern Europe. In none of these have the
original values experienced any such distur-
bance. Such a condition of things is so peculiar
to our language, it complicates the whole orthographic situation so thoroughly, that it demands first consideration in any discussion of
the various problems that need to be solved.

Let us give briefly, then, the most important facts in regard to the changes which have taken place in the history of these sounds.

II

MOVEMENT OF VOWEL-SOUNDS

The first vowel-sound of the alphabet—the *a* heard in *father* and *far*—has been aptly styled "the fundamental vowel-tone of the human voice." But the noticeable fact about it in English is that it has not only gone largely out of use already, but that it tends to go out of use more and more. Once the most common of articulate utterances, it has now become one of the rarest. In reducing the employment of it English has gone beyond all other modern cultivated tongues. The decline in its use has been steady. "In the Sanskrit," says Whitney, "in its long and short forms it makes over seventy per cent. of the vowels and about thirty per cent. of the whole alphabet." In examining his own utterance he rated the frequency of its occurrence at a little more than half of one per cent. This may be taken as fairly representative of the fortunes which have generally befallen the sound. Different parts of the English-speaking world preserve it, indeed, in different degrees. In Great Britain—if I can take as typical of all persons the pronunciation of it furnished to my own ears by a few—it is retained more fully than in the United States. But even there it has for a long period been disappearing. There is no reason to suppose that with our present orthography this process will not continue to go on.

The loss of this sound would assuredly be a great calamity to the speech. The coming of that day may be distant; it is to be hoped that it will never come at all. Yet owing to the incapacity of our orthography to represent pronunciation strictly, and therefore hold it fast permanently, the sound is certainly in danger of following to the very end the road on which it has long been travelling. It shows every sign of steady though slow disappearance. Once it was heard generally in many classes of words where it is now never heard at all. Such, for instance, was the case when *a* was followed by *n*, as in *answer, chance, dance, plant;* by *f*, as in *after;* by *s*, as in *grass, glass, pass;* by *st*, as in *last* and *vast.* More than a century ago the lexicographer Walker contended that this sound must formerly have been always heard in these and such like words, because it was "still the sound given to them by the vulgar, who are generally the last to alter the common pronunciation." There can be little doubt of the fact. In truth, Doctor Johnson distinctly specified *rather*, *fancy*, *congratulate*, *glass* among others as having it. Walker added that "the short *a* in these words"—those mentioned above—"is now the general pronunciation of the polite and learned world." Hence, he felt justified in asserting that the ancient sound "borders very closely on vulgarity."

This same result is showing itself in the instances where the vowel is followed by other letters or combinations of letters. Before *lf* and *th*—which can be illustrated respectively by *calf*, *half*, and by *path*, *bath*—the original sound, once generally heard, has given way largely and is still giving way. There are certainly many parts of the English-speaking world where the older pronunciation of it would be the exception and not the rule. The most effective agent in retaining it is a following *r*. In this case the sound is heard in no small number of words, as may be seen, for illustration, in *bar* and *car*. Another agency working for its retention, though far less powerful than the preceding, is a following *l*, as in *balm* and *calm*. But in this second case the sound is even now threatened with extinction. It exhibits in many places weakness of hold upon the utterance. Hence, it may come to take the road already trodden by other words in which it once showed itself. In the case of some of these, as a result of diminishing use, the sound, when heard, for illustration, in words like *half* and *calf*, is already looked upon by many as an affectation. Should such a feeling about it come not only to exist but to prevail when the vowel is followed by *lm*, its doom would be sealed. To hear *psalm* pronounced as the proper name *Sam* is still hateful to the orthoepically pure. Such a usage can as yet be politely termed a provincialism, or, insultingly, a vulgarism. Yet against the levelling tendency of an orthography which does not protect pronunciation, it is possible that the earlier sound of *a* in these words may not be able to hold out forever.

So much for the first vowel of the alphabet. We are as badly off, though in a different way, when we come to the second. It emphasizes the degeneracy which has overtaken our whole orthographic and orthoepic system that the name we now give to the first vowel was originally and still is scientifically the long sound of the second. The respective short and long values of this are heard in the words *met* and *mate*. In them are indicated the two sounds which the second vowel once had with us, and which it still retains in other cultivated tongues. The short sound continues to exist in all its primitive vigor, but the long sound is now very generally denoted by *a*. *E* itself no longer has it, save in the exclamation *eh*, and in certain cases where it is followed by *i* or *y*, such as *vein* and *rein*, and *they* or *obey*. Perhaps, indeed, it would be better to say that, strictly speaking, this letter by itself never indicates the sound at all; for the digraphs *ei* and *ey*, as we shall see later, have various distinct values, and are therefore entitled to be considered independently.

A condition of things not essentially dissimilar can be reported of the next vowel. Its original corresponding short and long sounds would be exactly represented by those heard in the words *fill* and *feel*. But the same transition or progression which has waited upon the second vowel has also attended the third. Its proper long sound has now become the name by which we regularly designate the second vowel. The fortunes of *i* have accordingly been about the same as those of its predecessor *e*. Here again the genuine short sound has been preserved in its integrity and on a large scale. But the letter is now only occasionally used to denote the long sound it had originally. This employment of it occurs too mainly in comparatively recent words of foreign origin. These have brought with them to a greater or less extent the pronunciation they had in the tongue from which they came. Some of the most common of these words are *caprice* and *police; fatigue* and *intrigue; profile; machine, magazine, marine,* and *routine;* and *antique, critique, oblique,* and *pique.* Once too it belonged to *oblige,* and even to this day the pronunciation *obleege* is occasionally heard.

What we call the third vowel is not a vowel, but a diphthong. We can see its sound and real character indicated in the Roman pronunciation of *Cæsar,* the German *kaiser,* or in the *ae* of the Spanish *maestro.* Against this general movement it can be said that the long and short sounds of the fourth vowel are much nearer their originals. This is by no means true, however, of the fifth. The genuine corresponding long and short sounds of it can be seen represented in the words *fool* and *full.* But we now almost universally apply the term "short *u*" to the neutral sound heard in *but* and *burn.* This sound occurs on the most extensive scale. It has, in fact, come to be one of the most common in our pronunciation, as to it all the vowels of

105

the unaccented syllables are disposed to tend. Even the sound of *u* in accented syllables begins to show occasional traces of this degeneration. Who has not heard that provincial pronunciation of the verb *put* which gives it the exact value of the initial syllable of *putty?* With nothing in our orthography to give fixity to orthoepy, there is little limit to the possibilities lying before this so-called "short *u*" in the way of displacing other sounds.

Let us now summarize the facts of the situation. The primal sound of the first vowel is on the road to complete disappearance. The long sound of the second vowel has usurped the name and in part the proper functions of the first. The long sound of the third vowel has performed a similar office for the second. The third vowel, so-called, is a diphthong. On the other hand, the short sounds of these three vowels—seen in *sat, set, sit*—continue to exist in their original integrity. All of them are employed on an extensive scale. Furthermore, the regular long and short sounds of *u* have no longer the prominence they once had in connection with this vowel. To the popular apprehension the idea of it is supplied, as has just been said, by the neutral vowel-sound we call "short *u*." This has largely taken the place of other vowel-sounds, and threatens to do so still more in the future.

The confusion in the use of the vowel-signs is itself reinforced by the condition of the alphabet. For the former, indeed, the latter is in no small measure responsible. Behind all the other agencies which have brought about the present wretched condition of our orthography stands out its one most glaring defect. The Roman alphabet we have adopted as our own is unequal to the demand made upon it. The three diphthongs being included in the consideration, we have at a low calculation fifteen vowel-sounds and but five characters to represent them. According to a more common calculation, we have eighteen vowel-sounds to be represented by this limited number. With the consonants we are a good deal better off. The supernumeraries being excluded, there are eighteen single characters for the twenty-four sounds to be denoted.

To make up for this deficiency of letters, two courses lay open to the users of English; rather, two courses were forced upon them. One was to have the same sign represent two or more sounds. This was at best a poor method of relief. Even had it been done correctly and systematically, so far as that result could be accomplished, it could not have failed to be unsatisfactory. It would have been an attempt to impose upon these few signs a burden they were unable to carry. But not even was this imperfect result achieved. Apparently it was not even aimed at. The sounds of the vowels have been so confused with one another that no fixed value can be attached to any vowel-sign. They are often used for each other in the most lawless fashion. So much is this the case that it is frequently impossible to tell from the spelling of a word what is the pronunciation of its vowel, or from the pronunciation of its vowel what is the spelling of the word.

There was another way followed to meet the difficulty. This second method was to make the best of the situation by that combination of vowels, or that combination of vowel and consonant, or of two consonants, to which we have given the name of digraphs. The first of these do not really constitute diphthongs, though such they have sometimes been termed. This method was far more sensible than the preceding. The task of making combinations of letters which should represent only particular sounds would have been, to be sure, a hard one. The lawlessness pervading our vowel - system would doubtless have prevented it from being carried

out with thoroughness. But carried out imperfectly, it would have been a distinct improvement upon what we have now. But so far from
any attempt having been made to accomplish it
on even an imperfect scale, it can hardly be
said to have been undertaken at all. There are
two instances, indeed, in which such combinations have an invariable or nearly invariable
value. One of these is *aw*, found in such words
as *bawl* and *lawn*. This digraph never has any
other sound than that of the so-called "broad
a"—heard, for illustration, in *fall* and *salt*. The
other is *ee*, seen in *seen* itself, as well as in a
number of other words. With two or three exceptions, this combination has that sound of the
third vowel we now ascribe to the second and
call "long *e.*" But in both these instances the
limitation of the digraph to the representation
of a single sound was a result of accident rather
than of design. These combinations were in
truth left to run the same haphazard course
which the letters composing them had usually
followed. Accordingly, to them extended the
lawlessness pervading the vowel-system. As a
consequence, the pronunciation of the numerous
digraphs became, as we shall see later, as varying and uncertain as that of the single vowels
themselves.

We come now to the consideration of specific
details upon which have been based the general
statements just made. Not by any means all
of them. There is no intention here of setting
forth an exhaustive enumeration of the facts
that could be presented. Even did I possess
the phonetic knowledge, which I lack, sufficient
to do this properly and fully, the undertaking
would have lain outside of my plan. Furthermore, it would hinder the effect of the argument for most persons rather than help it.
The mass of detail would be oppressive by its
volume, and for that very reason less impressive.
Accordingly, I throw out of consideration any
representation of the variations of pronunciation to be found in unaccented syllables. In
them indistinctness of sound, owing to the
inability of our present orthography to denote
precise values, has gone beyond that prevailing
in the other cultivated tongues of modern
Europe. Not only are the vowel-sounds in such
syllables pronounced differently by different individuals, they are pronounced differently by
the same individual at different times. In particular the precise pronunciation will be apt to
vary with the speaker's rapidity or slowness of
utterance. In one case the exact sound will
come out with perfect distinctness, in another

it will be hard to tell by what vowel it is represented. It is enough to say here of the unaccented syllables that there is a strong tendency, especially in hasty utterance, to give to them generally the sound of that neutral vowel we commonly call "short *u.*"

It is accordingly in these unaccented syllables that so many were wont to trip in the spelling contests once so popular. It was not unusual to have the very best equipped contestant fail. He attempted to use his reason; to succeed, it was essential to discard that and trust instead to his memory. Take, for illustration, so common a verb as *separate.* Who, ignorant of the word, could tell from the ordinary pronunciation of it—-even when that is reasonably distinct—what is the precise sound heard in the case of the second syllable? Should it be represented by an *a* or an *e?* The actual fact has to be learned, not through the agency of the ear, but through that of the eye. This is but a single instance out of hundreds that could be cited where a similar uncertainty must always prevail because the pronunciation cannot act as a clear guide to the present spelling.

In the following pages, therefore, attention shall be directed mainly to setting forth some of the most salient facts which reveal, in a way easily comprehensible, the confusion existing in our present orthography. For this purpose the discussion is intentionally confined almost entirely to those syllables upon which the principal accent falls. In a few instances some syllables will be included upon which rests the secondary accent. In both cases, however, the examples will be selected of words in which the distinction of sound is plainly apparent to all, and easily recognizable. This limits the discussion to but a section of the whole field. But though far from covering the ground, the absolute truth of the general statements about the condition of our orthography will appear distinctly manifest to him who has the patience to wade through the following dreary assemblage of facts, or perhaps it would be more proper to say, the following assemblage of dreary facts. Beginning with the vowel-system, the various letters or combinations of letters will be set forth which are used to indicate the same sound. In a number of instances these signs occur on a very small scale. Accordingly, three examples of every one will be invariably given when the sound heard is represented frequently by the spelling, or at least more or less frequently. When but one or two words are specified, this smaller number will denote that

these are all the ordinary ones of that class—
exclusive of derivatives and compounds—which
are known to exist. At any rate, they are all
that are known to exist to the writer. It is
not unlikely that examples have been overlooked which will suggest themselves to the
reader. We begin with the vowel-system.

III

THE VOWELS

The vowel *a* demands first attention. The
sound of it, heard in *father* and *far*, has been
spoken of as disappearing. The simple vowel
usually represents it, so far as it continues to
exist. Other signs, however, are occasionally
employed. It is heard in the *ua* of *guard* and
guardian, in the *ea* of *heart*, and also of *hearken*
when so spelled; and finally in England in the
e of *clerk*, *sergeant*, and a few other words. Once
much more common, it has even there steadily
given way before the advance of the so-called
"short *u*" sound, occurring in such words as *her*.
In the pronunciation of some it is further represented, for illustration, by the *au* of *haunt* and
haunch. On the other hand, as contrasted with
this declining use, the regular short sound of *a*,

heard in *man* and *mat*, is preserved in its fullest vigor. In the large majority of instances it is indicated by the simple letter itself. The exceptions to this representation of it are merely sporadic. Such are the *ua* of *guarantee* and the *ai* of *plaid*.

But dismissing the consideration of these two sounds of this vowel, take those heard respectively in the words *fare, fall,* and *fate*. Let us begin with the first of these. Its sound is denoted in many words by the simple vowel, as can be seen in *pare, care, declare*. But it is also indicated by *ai* in *pair, hair, stair;* by *ay* in *prayer;* by *e* in *there* and *where;* and by *ei* in *their* and *heir*. The second of these is the *au* sound heard in *all, warm, want*. It is not unfrequently denominated "broad *a*." But besides this vowel the sound is further represented by *o* in such words as *oft, loss, song;* by *au* in *daub, haul, taught,* and the like; similarly by *aw* in *saw, drawn, bawl,* and numerous others; by *oa* in *broad;* and by *ou* in *sought, thought, bought*.

It has already been pointed out that the so-called long sound of *a* does not strictly belong to it; that it is really an *e* sound. But as it has imposed its name upon the vowel, it is properly to be considered with it in any treatise which appeals to the general public. Its most usual representative is the letter itself, seen in *pale, pane, page,* and in scores of words in which the presence of an unpronounced final *e* has come to indicate generally, though not invariably, that the preceding vowel is long. But then again it is represented by *ai* in *pail, pain, exclaim;* by *ay* in *lay, pay, day;* by *ea* in *great, steak, break;* by *ei* in *veil, vein, heinous;* and by *ey* in *they, obey* and *survey.* In the interjection *eh* the vowel has for once its original sound. Again there are two instances in which a digraph with this sound occurs in but a single case. These two are the *ao* of *gaol* and the *au* of *gauge.*

In the case of the first of these words there were two ways of spelling it which existed from the fourteenth century. These are *gaol* and *jail.* The first form comes from the dialect of Normandy, the second from that of Paris. Both have been in use from the beginning. About both there has been to some extent controversy, at least in the past. The New Historical Dictionary, which contains a full history of the origin and use of these two forms, gives us a quotation bearing upon this point from Roger L'Estrange's translation of the *Visions of Quevedo.* In this version, which appeared in 1668, English allusions were not unfrequently

Introduced. In one instance men are represented as being in a state of rage because they cannot come to a resolution as to whether they ought to say *Goal* (*sic*) or *Jayl*. *Gaol* is still the official form of the word in England. That fact has mainly contributed to its maintenance in literature, so far as it continues to be used. In the United States *jail* is both the official and the literary form. But the spelling *gaol* has to some a peculiar attraction of its own. Not a single letter in it save the final *l* is of use in indicating with certainty its right pronunciation. In truth, the orthography almost enforces a wrong one. There are those to whom this fact is the highest recommendation it can have.

The second word has varied between the spellings *gauge* and *gage* almost from its very entrance into the language in the fifteenth century. One gets the impression that there was a time when the latter was the preferred form. But with our present knowledge no statement of this sort can be made positively. "You shall not gage me by what we do to-night," says Gratiano to Bassanio in *The Merchant of Venice*. Modern editions, in defiance of the original, print *gauge;* for the folio and both the early quartos agree in having *gage*. Shakespeare's use seems to be nothing but another

illustration of his perverse preference for the so-
called American spelling, or the American preference for Shakespeare's spelling, just as one
chooses to put it. Such an anomalous form as
gauge proved at times too much for the tolerance
of the orthographically much-enduring Englishman. Even him it has struck as peculiarly
objectionable. So in the eighteenth century he
set out to remove this particular blot upon the
speech. But as he was in nowise tainted with
the virus of reform, he exhibited the usual in-
curable aversion to having the spelling bear
any relation to the pronunciation. Accordingly,
he refused to take the natural as well as time-
honored course of dropping the unnecessary
and misleading *u*. Instead, he reversed the
order of the letters of the digraph. The *au*
became *ua*.

There have been in modern times men who
advocated this method of spelling the word with
all that fervor of faith which is so frequent an
accompaniment of limited knowledge. On this
point, for instance, the late Grant Allen felt
called upon to bear his testimony. He was
wont to make his novels a vehicle for conveying
his linguistic views as well as those pertaining
to religion, society, and politics. "Cynicus re-
plied, with an ugly smile," he wrote, "that

nobody could ever guage anybody else's nature," [1] Then, with what might fairly be called an ugly smile of his own, Allen added in a parenthesis, "not *gauge*, a vile dictionary blunder." There was no apparent reason for this lexical outburst; there was certainly no proof vouchsafed of the justice of the assertion. As the originals of the word were the Old French noun *gauge* and the verb *gauger*, it is hard to see how dictionaries could be held responsible for blunders, if blunders they were, which foreigners had perpetrated centuries before. There is, in truth, as little etymological justification for *guage* as there is phonetic for *gauge*. *Gage*, if it were not the most common way of spelling the word during the Elizabethan period, was certainly a common one. It is now, on the whole, the preferred form in the United States. Except in the nautical term *weather-gage*, the *u* is very generally retained in England. This is doubtless due to the desire of gratifying the ardent enthusiasm pervading the toiling millions of Great Britain for spellings which remind them of the Old French originals, from which were derived the words they employ.

In the case of the second vowel, the short *e*

---

[1] *Duchess of Powysland*, chap. **x.**

sound is properly shown in a large number of words of which *let, felt, bed* may be taken as representatives. These are all phonetically spelled. No educated man who saw them for the first time would have any hesitation about their pronunciation. Such a condition of things tends to chasten the feelings of that class of persons, not inconsiderable in number, who think it distinctively to the credit of the spelling that it should get as far away from the pronunciation as possible. They may be consoled, however, by the fact that this same sound is represented by *a* in *any* and *many;* by *ea* in a large number of words, such as *health, endeavor, weather;* by *ai* in *said* and *again;* by *ay* in *says;* by *ei* in *heifer* and *nonpareil,* and by *eo* in *jeopard* and *leopard.* There are those who give this short sound to *leisure,* ryming it with *pleasure,* as did Milton,[1] instead of the more common long sound heard with us. Indeed, it is noticeable that preference is given to the former in the New Historical English Dictionary, though that pronunciation is absolutely ignored in some of the best American ones. The compilers of these last may have been touched by

---

[1] And add to these retired leisure
That in trim garden takes his pleasure.
     —*Il Penseroso.*

Walker's pathetic plea for the long sound. *"Leisure,"* he wrote, "is sometimes pronounced as rhyming with *pleasure;* but in my opinion very improperly; for if it be allowed that custom is equally divided, we ought, in this case, to pronounce the diphthong long, as more expressive of the idea annexed to it."

Any and *many* are now the only two words where *a* has the sound of short *e.* At one time it was heard in others, and was not unfrequently so represented in literature. It lingers, too, in some instances, and even, indeed, flourishes in spite of all the efforts of education to extirpate it. The present authorized pronunciation of *catch,* instead of *ketch,* is one of the comparatively few triumphs gained by the written word over the spoken. In days when devotion did not exist to orthography irrespective of the purpose it was designed to fulfil, the *a* assumed the spelling of *e* along with its sound. The earlier *cag,* for illustration, has been abandoned for the pure phonetic spelling *keg.* Apparently no serious harm has befallen the language in consequence. Even more distant from the remote Latin original, *canalis,* denoting the home of *canis,* 'the dog,' is the form *kennel.* This turns its back upon its primitive, and contents itself with simply representing the pronunciation. So

much are we the creatures of habit and association in the matter of spelling that the most
ardent believer in the doctrine of basing orthography upon derivation could in neither of the
cases just mentioned be persuaded to revert to
the form nearest to that in the original tongue.

The sound to which we give the name of
"long *e*" belongs strictly, as has been pointed
out, to *i*. A few of the words have also been
given in which it still continues to be so indicated.[1] There are certain conditions under
which it is represented by the simple letter itself. One is when it alone constitutes an accented syllable, as in *equal, era, ecliptic.* Another
when it ends a monosyllable or an accented
syllable, as in *he, be, regal, cohesion.* It appears
finally with a good deal of frequency in words
in which the sound of the simple vowel is
lengthened by the artificial device of an appended mute *e*, as in *theme, precede, complete.*
This last word, it may be said in passing, was
once often spelled *compleat.* But as the letter
itself represents much more usually the short
sound of the vowel, the long sound has come
to be indicated often by various digraphs. Of
these, two are particularly prominent. One of

[1] See page 105

121

them is *ee*, seen in a large number of words, such
as *meet, thee, proceed.* The second digraph is *ea*,
found in *bean, meat, eagle,* and a host of others.
But the sound is not limited to these two combinations. It is represented by *ei* in *receive,
conceit, seize;* by *ie* in *believe, chief, fiend;* by
ey in *key;* by *eo* in *people;* by *ay* in *quay;* by
æ in *ægis, pæan, minutiæ;* and several other
words not fully naturalized.

Once, indeed, this last method of indicating
the sound was far more common. In many
instances it has been supplanted by the simple
e. It was not till a comparatively late period
that such spellings as *era* and *ether* drove out in
great measure the once prevalent *æra* and
æther. As *æ* has with us strictly but one sound,
the change cannot, from all points of view, be
deemed an improvement. In the case of an
unknown word first brought to the attention,
no one could now be positive, under certain conditions, whether the vowel should be treated as
long or short. Take, for illustration, *encyclo-
pedia,* once often spelled *encyclopædia.* He who
sees the word for the first time is as likely to
pronounce the antepenultimate syllable *pĕd* as
pēd. He certainly could not tell from the
orthography employed how this particular
syllable should be sounded. Still, for much more

than a century the tendency of the users of the language has been steadily directed toward the discarding of the *œ* in all cases. As long ago as 1755 Dr. Johnson, in his dictionary, recommended its disuse. "*Æ*," he wrote, "is sometimes found in Latin words not completely naturalized or assimilated, but is by no means an English diphthong, and is more properly expressed by single *e*, as *Cesar, Eneas*." Dr. Johnson was hostile to spelling reform; but he could venture to sanction a spelling of these two Latin proper names, at which even the average spelling reformer would shudder.

Fortunately for those of us who believe that spelling exists for the sake of indicating pronunciation, the sound of short *i*, one of the most common vowel sounds in the language, is almost always represented by the letter itself. The exceptions are few, comparatively speaking. The only sign to take its place in any body of words sufficiently numerous to be entitled a class is *y*, as seen in *syntax, abyss, system,* and other words, generally of Greek origin. The instances where different signs are employed are purely sporadic. Most of them, however, are for various reasons remarkable. The sound is represented by *e* in the name of the language we speak and of the country where it came into being. It is further represented by the *e* of *pretty*, by the *o* of *women*, by the *u* of *busy* and *business*, by the *ie* of *sieve*, and by the *ui* of *guild* and *guilt* and *build*. Once in the speech of most men, and now in that of many, it is given to the *ee* of *been*, and regularly to that combination as found in *breeches*.

Gild is a variant spelling of *guild*, and represents the earlier form. The *ui* of the two additional examples given ought to be a saddening spectacle to the devout believer in derivation as the basis of orthography. The original form of *guilt* was *gylt*. So it remained with various spellings—of which *gilt* was naturally the most common—until the sixteenth century. But there was also an allied form, *gult*. These two undoubtedly represented distinct and easily recognizable pronunciations of the word. They were at last combined so as to create a spelling, of the pronunciation of which no one could now be certain until he was told. This did not take place on any scale worth mentioning until the latter part of the sixteenth century, though the combination had occasionally been seen much earlier. Essentially the same thing can be said of *build*. It originally appeared in various ways, of which *byld*, *bild*, and *buld* were the prominent types. At the end of the fifteenth

124

century the practice began of recognizing both forms by writing *build* or *buyld*. In a measure this doubtless represented a then existing shade of pronunciation. The spelling, once established, has continued since. No one ever thinks of pronouncing the *u;* perhaps no one has ever thought of it since the combination was formed. Yet there is no question that intense sorrow would be occasioned to a certain class of persons were they to be deprived of the pleasure of inserting in the word this useless and now orthoepically misleading letter.

The so-called "long *i*" ought strictly to be treated under the diphthongs; but as it is popularly associated in the minds of men with the simple vowel, its diphthongal sound will be considered at this point. Its most usual representative is the letter itself. This presents little difficulty in the pronunciation if the words end with a mute *e*, as in *mine, desire, bite*. The distinction between *thin* and *thine,* for instance, is then easily made. But when it comes to such words as *mind, child,* and *pint* on the one hand, and *lift, gild,* and *tint* on the other, there is nothing in the spelling to indicate with certainty how the *i* of these words should be sounded. As no general rule can be laid down, the pronunciation of each has in consequence to be learned by itself. This uncertainty was perhaps one of the causes which led to the transition of the diphthongal sound of *i* in *wind* to the short sound *wĭnd*, which so aroused the wrath of Dean Swift. But besides *i* the sound is also indicated by the *y* of *type, ally, thyme,* and a number of words derived from the Greek; by *ie*, especially in monosyllables, such as *die, lie,* and *tie;* by *ye* in the noun *lye;* by *ei* in *height* and *sleight,* and according to one method of pronunciation in *either* and *neither.* It is further represented by the *ai* of *aisle,* by the *ey* of *eye,* and by the *uy* of *buy.*

The third vowel now demands attention. Orthoepists contend that there is no genuine short *o* in English utterance. Without entering into a discussion of this point. it is sufficient to say that the two sounds of the letter, which are ordinarily designated as short and long, are represented respectively in the words *not* and *note.* The former sound remains fairly faithful to this vowel. It is hardly indicated by any other sign. The *a* of *what, squad, quarry* is about the only one to take its place. Very different is it with the long sound heard in *note.* This is far from confining itself to any single letter. In no small number of words it is represented by *oa*, as in *boat, groan, coal;* by *oe*, as in *foe, toe, hoe;* by

ou, as in *pour*, *mould*, *shoulder;* or again by
ow, as seen in *crow*, *snow*, *show*. Less common,
but still to be met with, is this sound heard
in the combination *ew*, as seen in *sew;* as well
as in *shew* and *strew*, as these words were once
regularly and are now occasionally spelled;
in *oo*, as in *door* and *floor;* in *eau*, in *beau*,
bureau, and *flambeau;* and in the *eo* of *yeoman*.

This last word was once spelled at times
yoman and at times *yeman*. These forms
doubtless represented the two ways of pronouncing it that existed. The *Toxophilus* of
Roger Ascham, for illustration, was dedicated
to the use "of the gentlemen and yomen of
Englande." But the sound of the vowel of the
first syllable wavered for a long period between
the long *o* and the short *e*. Ben Jonson, in the
earlier part of the seventeenth century, observed
of the word that "it were truer written *yĕman*."
In the latter half of the eighteenth century Doctor Johnson tells us that the *eo* of this word
"is sounded like *e* short." This was the view
taken by perhaps the larger number of orthoepists, who immediately followed him. In spite
of them the *o* pronunciation has triumphed.
It has shown, however, a tender consideration
for its defeated rival by allowing it to lead a

useless existence in the syllable in which, in the utterance of many, it once represented the actual sound.

The corresponding short and long sounds of *u* are seen in the words *full* and *rule*. But *o*, either singly, or in combination with other letters, is a favorite way of indicating both. The short sound of this vowel, which is far from common, is represented by the *o* of *bosom*, *woman, wolf;* by the *oo* of *good, foot, stood;* by the *ou* of *could, would, should.* On the other hand, the corresponding long sound is also represented by the *o* of *move, prove, lose;* by the *oe* of *shoe* and *canoe;* by the *oo* of *too, root, fool;* by *ou* in such words as *uncouth, routine, youth,* and a number of others derived generally from the French. There has been and still is something of a tendency on the part of the users of language to change the long sound of *oo* into its short one. Oliver Wendell Holmes, in his poem of *Urania*, represents Learning as giving a lesson on propriety of pronunciation. Among other points considered, occurred the following observations:

She pardoned one, our classic city's boast,
That said at Cambridge mŏst instead of mōst.
But knit her brows and stamped her angry foot
To hear a Teacher call a rōot a rŏot.

SPELLING REFORM

This is perhaps as good an example as can be furnished of the waste of time and labor imposed by our present orthography in mastering distinctions of sounds in words when there is nothing in the sign employed to indicate which one is proper. To men not given up to slavish admiration of our present spelling, it would seem that Learning, instead of stamping her foot, would have been much more sensibly engaged in using her head to devise some method by which one and the same combination of letters should not be called upon to represent two distinct sounds in words so closely allied in form as *foot* and *root;* or distinct sounds in words with the same ending as *toe* and the *shoe* that covers it.

Another way of indicating the long sound of this vowel is either by the simple letter itself or by it in combination with other letters. For instance, it is represented by *ue* in such words as *true, avenue, pursue;* by *ui* in *fruit, bruise, pursuit;* by *eu* in *neuter, deuce, pentateuch;* by *ew* in *brew, sewer, lewd;* and by *ieu* in *adieu, lieu, purlieu.* But there is a peculiarity in the words containing this vowel, the consideration of which involves too much space to have little more than a reference here. We all recognize the difference of the sound of *u* as heard respectively in *fortune* and *fortuitous*, in *annual* and *annuity*, in *volume* and *voluminous*, in *penury* and *penurious*. In the first one of each of these pairs of words a *y*-element is introduced into the pronunciation; in the second the *u* has its absolutely pure long sound. Nor is this introduction of the *y*-element limited to the letter when used alone. We can find it exemplified in the *ue* of *statue, value, tissue;* in the *eu* of *eulogy, euphony, Europe;* in the *ew* of *ewe, hew, few*. This iotization, as it is called, is especially prevalent in words with the termination *ture*, as *nature, furniture, sculpture,* and *agriculture*. Now and then some one is heard giving, or attempting to give, to the *u* of this ending the pure sound; but such persons are usually regarded as possessed of "cultoor" and not culture.

The only word of this special class in which such a method of pronunciation can be said to have attained any recognition whatever is *literature*. The word itself is an old one in our speech. Once, however, it meant merely knowledge of literature. It did not mean that body of writings which constitute the production of a country or of a period. This sense of it, now the most common, is comparatively modern. The earliest instance I have chanced to meet of it—though it was doubtless used a good deal earlier—is in the correspondence of Southey and William Taylor of Norwich. There it occurs in a letter belonging to the year 1803, in which Southey tells his friend that he was expecting to undertake the editorship of a work dealing biographically and critically with "the history of English literature." [1] Still, the pronunciation just mentioned of this word, differing as it does from the others of the same class, must even then have been occasionally heard. It was certainly made the subject of comment by Byron. He somewhere speaks—I have mislaid the reference—of a publisher who was in the habit of talking about *literatoor*. This peculiar pronunciation still comes at times from the lips of educated men.

But the regular long and short sounds of *u* yield in frequency of occurrence to that sound of it heard in *but* and *burn*. In common speech this has usurped with us the title of "short *u*." By orthoepists it itself is divided into a long and a short sound, according as it is or is not followed by an *r*. Into it, as has been pointed out, the pronunciation of all unaccented syllables tends to run. Hence, in the case of these,

[1] *Memoir of the Life and Writings of the late William Taylor of Norwich*. London, 1843. Southey to Taylor, July 13, 1803, vol. i, p. 466.

there has come to exist the greatest possible variety of signs by which it is indicated. But even in the accented syllables there is a sufficient number of different ones to arrest the attention. Naturally the most usual representative of it is the vowel from which it has taken its name. But it is far from being limited to this sign. Its short sound is further represented by the *o* of such words as *love*, *dove*, and *son;* similarly by the *ou* of *double*, *touch*, and *young;* and by the *oo* of *blood* and *flood*. In vulgar speech *soot* would have to be added to the last two. Furthermore, it is represented by the sporadic example of the *oe* of *does*. The long sound runs through a still wider range of examples. Words containing it but denoted by various signs could be given by the score. It is represented by all the vowels except the first. The *e* of *her*, *were*, *fern*, stands for it. So does the *i* of *fir*, *bird*, *virgin*. So does the *o* of *work*, *worship*, *worth*. It is likewise largely represented by *ea* in such words as *heard*, *learn*, *search;* by *ou* in *scourge*, *journal*, *flourish*, and no small number of others containing this particular sign. In the single instance of *tierce* the sound is denoted also by *ie*. Were its use in unaccented syllables indicated, this list of signs would be largely extended. As it is, it will be seen that nine is the

132

number employed in accented syllables to represent it.

So much for the simple vowels. We come now to the three diphthongs. The first of these, which is made up of the sound of the *a* of *father* and that of the *e* of *they*, has already been considered in treating what is called "long *i*." Eight signs were given by which it was denoted.[1] This wealth of representation does not belong to the two other diphthongs. There are but two signs by which the sound of the second is indicated. These are the *ou* of *south, found, about*, and the *ow* of *now, town, vowel*. The third diphthong again has but two signs, the *oi* of *boil, point, spoil*, and the *oy* of *boy, joy, destroy*. Many of the words in which *oi* appears had once the pronunciation of the first mentioned diphthong. To the truth of this both the rymes of the poets and the assertions of the early orthoepists bear ample testimony. The statement is still further confirmed by the fact that the sound still lingers, or, rather, is prevalent, in the speech of the uneducated, the great conservators of past usage. The words given above as illustrative of this sign of the diphthong would have been pronounced by our fathers

[1] See page 125

bīle, pīnt, spīle. So they are still pronounced by the illiterate. In one word, indeed, this sound has not passed entirely from the colloquial speech of the cultivated either in England or America. *Roil* is not merely heard as *rīle*, but is not unfrequently found so printed.

IV

THE DIGRAPHS

Up to this point we have been engaged in making manifest the numerous different ways in which the same vowel-sound is represented in our present orthography. Necessarily a reversal of the process would present an equally impressive showing, for examples just as impressive would make manifest how the same sign adds to the further confusion of English spelling by denoting a number of different vowel-sounds. But there is a limit to the endurance of the reader, to say nothing of that of the writer. Furthermore, there is little need of this addition in the case of the vowels. The facts about to be furnished will be more than sufficient to satisfy any demand for illustrations of the extent to which the same sign has been made to indicate a wide variety of differ-

ent sounds, though in the sporadic instances the
examples already given must be repeated. For
we come now to the consideration of those combinations of letters, numerous in English spelling,
to which has been given the name of digraphs.
They are sometimes made up of a union of vowels, sometimes of a union of a vowel and a consonant, sometimes of a union of two consonants.

I have already adverted to the fact that had
there been any system established in the employment of these combinations of letters, and
had each of them been made to represent un-
varyingly one particular sound, some of the
worst evils of English orthography would have
been largely mitigated, and in certain cases entirely relieved. But this was not to be. The
opportunity of bringing about regularity of
usage in the employment of these signs was
either not seen, or if seen was not improved.
The same variableness, the same irregularity,
the same lawlessness which existed in the representation of the sounds of the vowels and diphthongs came to exist in the case of the digraphs
also. They consequently did little more than
add to the confusion prevailing in English orthography, and became as valueless for indicating pronunciation as are the single letters of
which they are composed.

To this sweeping statement there are two partial exceptions. The first is *aw*. This is one of several representatives of the so-called broad sound of *a* heard in *ball* and *fall*. Whenever that digraph appears, its pronunciation is invariably the same. No such absolute assertion can be made of the digraph which represents the sound of "long *e*." This is the combination *ee*. There are but two exceptions in common use to the pronunciation of it just given. The first is the word *breeches*. Its singular has the regular sound. The pronunciation as short *i* in the plural—used, too, there in a special sense—may perhaps be due to an extension to this form of that tendency, so prevalent in English speech, on the part of the derivative, to shorten the vowel of the primitive. The other is the participle *been* of the substantive verb. In usage the pronunciation of this word has long wavered and still wavers between the sounds heard respectively in *sin* and *seen*. Of this variation there will be occasion to speak later in detail.

These exceptions, however, affect but a limited number of words. They are hardly worth considering when their regularity is put in contrast with the irregularities of the other combinations. Let us begin with the digraph *ai.* Ordinarily it has the sound we are accustomed to call "long *a*," as can be seen in *fail*, *rain*, and *paid*. In *pair*, *fair*, *hair* it has another sound. In *said*, *again*, *against* it has the sound of short *e*. In *aisle* it has the diphthongal sound called by us "long *i*." This word furnishes an interesting illustration of the way in which much of our highly prized orthography came to have a being. Its present spelling is comparatively recent. Doctor Johnson recognized in it the lack of conformity to any possible derivation. He adopted it on the authority of Addison, though with manifest misgiving. He thought it ought to be written *aile*, but in deference to this author he inserted it in his dictionary as *aisle*.

"Thus," he said, "the word is written by Addison, but perhaps improperly." [1] Johnson's action was followed without thought and without hesitation by his successors. There is no question, indeed, as to the impropriety of the present spelling from the point of view of both derivation and pronunciation. Equally there is no doubt as to the impropriety of its meaning from the former point of view. It came re-

[1] "The church is one huge nef with a double Aisle to it."—Addison, *Remarks on Several Parts of Italy, etc.* First edition, 1705, p. 493.

137

motely from the Latin *ala*, 'a wing.' Therefore, it means really the wing part of the church
on each side of the nave. In this sense it is
still employed. But since the first half of the
eighteenth century it has been made to denote
also the passage between rows of seats. Strictly
speaking, this is a particularly gross corruption,
though, like so many in our speech, it has now
been sanctioned by good usage. The proper
word to indicate such a sense was *alley*, corresponding to the French *allée*, 'a passage.'
This was once common and is still used in the
North of England. *Aisle* itself was formerly
spelled *ile* or *yle*. Confusing it with *isle*, originally spelled *ile*, men inserted an *s* about the end
of the seventeenth century. Later an *a* was
prefixed under the influence of the French *aile*.
It was thus that this linguistic monster, defying
any correct orthography or orthoepy, was created. In any sense of it the *s* is an unjustifiable
intrusion, representing as the word does in one
signification the Latin *ala*, 'a wing,' and in the
other the French *allée*, 'a passage.'

There is another word containing this digraph
which illustrates vividly the uncertainty of
sound caused by the present spelling. This is
plait, both as verb and substantive. About its
pronunciation usage has long been conflicting.

"*Plait*, a fold of cloth, is regular, and ought to be pronounced like *plate*, a dish," said Walker, at the beginning of the eighteenth century. "Pronouncing it so as to rhyme with *meat*," he added, "is a vulgarism, and ought to be avoided." So say several later English dictionaries. So say the leading American ones. Webster, indeed, concedes that the pronunciation denounced by Walker is colloquially possible. It therefore does not necessarily relegate the user of it to the ranks of the vulgar. Now comes the New Historical English Dictionary, and gives the word not merely three distinct pronunciations, but holds up as only really proper that which has failed to gain the favor of most lexicographers. It is the one found "in living English use," it says, when the word has the sense of 'fold.' Further we are assured that with this signification it is ordinarily written *pleat*. This would tend to justify still more the ryme with *meat*, which so shocked Walker. Then in its second sense of a 'braid of hair or straw' we are told that it has the sound of *a* in *mat*. This leaves the pronunciation of *plait* to ryme with *plate* hardly any support to stand on. It has merely the distinction of being mentioned first; but it is denied a real existence as a spoken word. Nothing could better illustrate the unlimited possibilities opened by our present orthography for discussions of propriety of pronunciation about which certainty can never be assured. All statements about general usage, no matter from what source coming, must necessarily be received with a good many grains of allowance, if not with a fair proportion of grains of distrust—at least, whenever our orthoepic doctors disagree. Do the best the most conscientious investigator can, he can never make himself familiar with the practice of but a limited number of educated men who have a right to be consulted. His conclusions, therefore, must always rest upon a more or less imperfect collection of facts.

The digraph *ay* is naturally subject to the same influences as *ai*. It is, however, much less used save at the end of words. Grief has, indeed, been felt and expressed, even by devout worshippers of our present orthography, at the arbitrary change of signs made in the inflection of certain verbs, like *lay*, *pay*, *say*. These, without any apparent reason for so doing, pass from the digraph *ay* in the present to *ai* in the preterite. Naturally there is no objectionable uniformity in the practice. That might tend to render slightly easier the acquisition of our spelling. Accordingly, *lay* and *pay* and *say* have in the past tense *laid*, *paid*, and *said*, while verbs with the same termination, such as *play*, *pray*, *delay*, have in this same past tense the forms *played* and *prayed* and *delayed*. *Stay* uses impartially *staid* and *stayed*. Much dissatisfaction has been expressed at the "wanton departure from analogy," as it has been called, which has been manifested by the words of the first list given. As the characteristic of our spelling everywhere is a wanton departure from analogy, it hardly seems worth while to find fault with this particular exhibition of it.

In *quay* the digraph has the entirely distinct sound of "long *e*." Of this word it may be added that the spelling is modern while the pronunciation is ancient. Originally it appeared as *key* or *kay*—of course, with the usual orthographic variations. In the earlier half of the eighteenth century, under the influence of the French *quai*, the present form of the word came in; toward the end of the century it had become the prevailing form. This gave the lexicographer, Walker, an opportunity to display his hostility to any sort of spelling which should engage in the reprehensible task of aiming to indicate pronunciation. Such a proceeding was in his eyes a radically vicious course of

action. In the entire ignorance of the original
form of the word he remarked that it "is now
sometimes seen written *key;* for if we cannot
bring the pronunciation to the spelling, it is
looked upon as some improvement to bring the
spelling to the pronunciation—a most pernicious
practice in language."

Key, as the spelling suggests, had originally
the sound of *ey* in *they* and *obey;* later it passed
into the sound of "long *e*." This it has transmitted to its supplanter. In the scarcity of
rymes in our tongue, it is always a little venture-
some to infer from the evidence of verse the
past pronunciation of words which have with
us the same termination, but different sounds.
This imparts a little uncertainty to the treatment of *quay* in two passages containing the word
which are given by the New Historical Dictionary.

> But now arrives the dismal day
> She must return to Ormond-quay,

says Swift in his poem of *Stella at Wood-Park.*
Does the ryme here represent an attempt
to conform the pronunciation to the spelling?
More likely it represents the survival of a pronunciation once more or less prevalent. The
second extract from *In Memoriam* is under the
circumstances more striking:

> If one should bring me the report
>   That thou hadst touched the land to-day,
>   And I went down unto the quay,
> And found thee lying in the port.

It certainly looks as if in this passage Tennyson had set out to make the pronunciation conform to the spelling.

Our next digraph is *ea.* This has a choice variety of sounds to represent. Most commonly it receives the pronunciation of "long *e.*" Of the scores of examples containing it, *beast, hear,* and *deal* may be taken as specimens. But while this is its most frequent sound, it is far from being the only one. Its most important rival is that of short *e,* which can be found in no small number of words like *breath, breast, weather.* In these and all other like cases the second vowel is absolutely superfluous as regards pronunciation. The unnecessary letter is in some instances due to derivation; in others it exists in defiance of it—as, for instance, in *feather* and *endeavor.* Its insertion was doubtless due to an attempt to represent a sound which is no longer heard in these words. In a large number of instances they were once spelled without the now unpronounced letter.

Common also is a third sound of this digraph —the one we call "short *u.*" It is heard in *heard* itself, in *earth*, in *early*, in *learn*, in *search*, and in a number of other words in which *ea* is followed by *r*. There is a fourth sound of it which may be represented by *bear*, *swear*, *tear*. A fifth sound of it occurs in the words *heart*, *hearth*, and *hearken*. Again, a sixth sound of it is represented by such words as *great*, *break*, *steak*. In all these cases it will be observed that certain of these words have in the course of their history tended to pass from one pronunciation of the digraph into another. Sometimes they have for a long time wavered between the two. *Hearth*, which contains the fifth sound just assigned to the combination, was often made to ryme with words containing the third sound, represented by *earth*. According to the New Historical Dictionary, this is true now of Scotland, and of the Northern English dialect. It is true also of certain parts of the United States, or, at any rate, of certain persons. It seems also to have been the pronunciation of Milton.

> Far from all resort of mirth
> Save the cricket on the hearth

are lines found in *Il Penseroso*. So also *great* once had often the first sound here given to the digraph, as if it were spelled *greet*. Both this sound as well as the one it now receives were so equally authorized in the eighteenth century that Dr. Johnson triumphantly cited the fact as a convincing proof of the impossibility of making a satisfactory pronouncing dictionary, just as we are now told that we cannot have a phonetic orthography because men pronounce the same word in different ways.

The digraph *ee* having already been considered, we pass on to *ei*. Its most frequent sound is that heard in such words as *rein, veil*, and *neighbor*. But it has also the sound of "long *e*" in *conceit, seize, ceiling*, and a few others. In *heir* and *heiress* and *their* it has the sound of *a* in *fare*. In *height* and *sleight* it has the sound of "long *i*." In *heifer* and *nonpareil* it has the sound of short *e*. The allied digraph *ey* has no such range of sounds. In accented syllables it represents only the first one given to *ei*, as can be seen in *they, grey*, and *survey*. *Key*, with the sound of "long *e*," seems to be the solitary exception.

It is already plainly apparent that there is nothing in the character of our present spelling to fit it to serve as a guide to pronunciation, the very office for which spelling was created. But its worthlessness in this respect, with the consequent uncertainty and anxiety attending the use of it, forms in the case of two words containing the digraph *ei*, one of the most amusing episodes in the history of English orthoepy. In modern times their pronunciation has given rise to controversy and heart-burnings as bitter as the matter itself is unimportant. These words are *either* and *neither*. Were they to adopt the most common pronunciation of the digraph they would have the sound heard in such words as *eight, vein,* and *feint*. This, in truth, they once had. To indicate that fact they have occasionally been written *ayther* and *nayther*. But this pronunciation, outside of Ireland at least, had largely disappeared by the latter part of the eighteenth century. So far as many orthoepists were concerned, it was ignored entirely. Those who mentioned it often accorded it scant favor. The affections of lexicographers were long divided between the sounds heard in *receive* and *deceit*, and that heard in *height* and *sleight*. For the former there was a very marked preference. Most of them did not even admit the existence of the "long *i*" sound; those who did, gave it generally a grudging recognition. The various pronunciations prevailing in the latter part of the eighteenth century were specified by Nares in his *Elements of Orthoepy*. "*Either* and *neither,*" he wrote, "are spoken by some with the sound of long *i.* I have heard even that of long *a* given to them; but as the regular way is also in use, I think it is preferable. These differences seem to have arisen from ignorance of the regular sound of *ei.*" As the regular sound of *ei,* if any one of them is entitled to that designation, is heard in such words as *skein* and *freight,* one gets the impression that Nares himself was ignorant of what it was.

Walker, the orthoepic lawgiver of our fathers, distinctly preferred the "long *e*" sound of *either* and *neither.* Both the practice of Garrick and analogy led him to maintain that they should be pronounced as if ryming "with breather, one who breathes." He was compelled, however, to admit that the "long *i*" sound was heard so frequently that it was hardly possible in insist exclusively upon the other. He did the best he could, nevertheless, to ignore it and thereby banish it. While in the introduction to his dictionary he recognized the existence of both sounds, in the body of his work that of "long *e*" was the only one given. In this course he was followed by his reviser, Smart, who succeeded to his name, and up to a certain degree to his authority. Smart went even

147

further than his predecessor. He was apparently ignorant of the fact—he certainly ignored it
—that any other pronunciation of these words
than that of "long *e*" was known to the English people. But in spite of its defiance of
analogy and of the hostility of lexicographers,
the sound of "long *i*" continued to make its
way. The fact has sometimes excited the indignation of orthoepists. Yet it is hard to
understand how any one who cherishes the
vagaries of English spelling should get into a
state of excitement about the vagaries of its
pronunciation.

Neither the digraph *eo* nor *eu* is found often.
The first, however, improves fully the opportunity presented of making it difficult, if not
impossible, for the learner to get any idea of
the pronunciation from the spelling. In *people*
it has the sound of "long *e*"; in *leopard* and
jeopard it has the sound of short *e*. In *yeoman*
again it has the sound of long *o*. *Eu* has practically the same sound as *ew*, as can be exemplified in *feud* and *few*. This last digraph, however, represents the long sound of *u* as well as
that in which iotization precedes the vowel.
The difference in the pronunciation of *drew* and
dew will make manifest the contrast. There is
always a tendency, however, for the digraph to

pass from the latter sound to the former in a tongue in which there is nothing in the orthography to fix a precise value upon the sign indicating both. "According to my v'oo," Oliver Wendell Holmes, in his *Elsie Venner*, has one of his characters saying. "The unspeakable pronunciation of this word," he adds in a parenthesis, "is the touchstone of New England Brahminism." In another place in the same novel he still further enforces this point. "The Doctor," he wrote, among his other recommendations to the hero, says to him, "you can pronounce the word *view*." And yet in it the iotization is plainly indicated by the vowel itself, while in such words as *hew* and *few* and *new* there is nothing to fix definitely the sound. Finally, it remains to say of this digraph that *shew* and *strew*, two verbs once spelled with it, have now become *show* and *strow*, a form more in accordance with their pronunciation. There is no particular reason why *sew* should not follow their example in substituting an *o* for an *e*.

The digraph *ie* is represented but by three vowel sounds. The most common one is that of "long *e*"—seen, for example, in *chief, grieve, believe*. But the sound of "long *i*" is heard in no small number of words, especially monosyllabic words ending in *ie*, such as *lie, die, tie*.

In one instance it has the sound of short *e*. Accordingly, in it the first vowel is distinctly superfluous. This is the word *friend*. Its Anglo-Saxon original is *freónd*, just as that of *fiend* is *feónd* or *fiónd*. One of the small jokes of the opponents of spelling reform is a professed unwillingness "to knock the eye out of a friend." Disparaging remarks have been made about this as an argument—as it seems to me, with no justification. Compared with most of the objections brought against the efforts to wash the dirty face of our orthography and make it decently presentable, this particular argument against dropping the *i* out of *friend* is, as I look at it, the strongest that has been or can be adduced. It reminds one, indeed, of the objection the French writer made to the dropping of the *h* out of *rhinoceros*. The animal would lose his horn and become nothing more than a sheep.

As a matter of linguistic history, however, it was not until late in the sixteenth century that the *i*, though found long before, appeared in the word *friend* to an extent worth considering. There were several ways in which it had been spelled previously. Of these *frend* was naturally a common one in days when the belief still lingered that the office of orthography was to represent pronunciation and not to get as far away from it at possible. Take, as an illustration, the treatise entitled *The Schoolmaster* of the great English scholar, Roger Ascham. This appeared in 1570. In it the word *friend* occurs just twenty five times. It is regularly spelled *frend*, with the exception of one instance, where the intruding *i* is found. So also *frendly* is invariably the form of the adjective, and *frendship* that of the derivative noun.[1]

Oa, the next digraph in order, comes very near attaining the distinction of being represented by a single sound. It occurs in a fairly large number of words which can be represented by *oar*, *coat*, *loaf*. It is saved, however, from the reproach of regularity by having the sound of the *a* of "ball" in the words *broad*, *abroad*, and *groat*. *Oe* is not so common, but, like its reverse *eo*, what it lacks in number of words it makes up in variety of pronunciation. In *foe*,

[1] In Professor Arber's accurate reprint of the original edition, the word, spelled as *frend*, can be found on pages, 20, 21, 22, 24, 43, 73, 75, 87, 89, 90, 91, 94, 99, 113, 121, 140, 149, 154, and 158. In some instances the word appears two or more times on the page. On pages 23 (twice) and 113 is found *frendly*, and on page 140 *frendship*. Nowhere does the *i* appear in these last two words. The solitary instance of the spelling *friend* is on page 112.

hoe, and *toe* it has the sound of long *o*. In *canoe* and *shoe* it has the sound of long *u*. In these instances it forms the termination of words. Not so in *does*, where it has the sound we call "short *u*." The use of this digraph, like that of *ae*, has been much restricted. For instance, the word we now spell *fetid* was once generally spelled *fœtid*. So, in truth, it continued to be till the nineteenth century. The digraph, indeed, still lingers in the name of the drug *asafœtida*, though in the instance of this word the long sound has given way to the short. Not unlike, in some particulars, has been the fortune of certain other terms. Take, for instance, the word *economy*. Its remote Greek original began with *oi*, which in English, as in Latin, appeared with the form *œ*, and sometimes erroneously *æ*. For these was found occasionally the simple *e*. In the nineteenth century this last displaced the two others, and gave to the first syllable the present standard form. One of the results, however, of this sort of substitution is that no one seems to be certain whether he ought to pronounce the initial *e* of *economic* as long or short.

The ordinary sound of *oo*, the next digraph to be considered, is that of long *u*, as we see it in *moon, soon, food*. But there are about half a dozen words—throwing derivatives out of consideration—in which it has the short sound of *u*. The difference can be plainly observed by contrasting the pronunciation of the digraph in the two words *mood* and *wood*. Furthermore, *oo* is to be credited with two more sounds. One is that of the "short *u*" seen in *blood* and *flood*. The other is the long sound of *o* in *door* and *floor*, anciently spelled *dore* and *flore*. *Dore*, for instance, can be found in Chaucer, Shakespeare, Milton, and even as late as Bunyan.

The digraph *ou* is perhaps the banner sign for the frequency of its occurrence and the variety of sounds it indicates. As it appears most commonly, it is a genuine diphthong, as seen in such words as *loud*, *sour*, *mouth*. But there is another large body of words in which the sign has a sound essentially distinct. It can be observed in such words as *group*, *youth*, *tour*. It gives one a peculiar idea of the worth of English orthography as a guide to pronunciation that in *thou*, the singular of the pronoun of the second person, *ou* has one value, and in its plural, *you*, it has a value altogether different. The same observation is true of the possessives *our* and *your*. There are two or three words in which these two signs have had for a long period a struggle for the ascendancy.

Take the case of the substantive *wound*. One gets the impression from poetry that in this word the *ou* constitutes a genuine diphthong. There is no question that it rymes regularly with words containing the diphthongal sound here given. Perhaps that was a necessity; it had to ryme with such or not ryme at all. Still, the verse seems pretty surely to have represented the common pronunciation. In the couplets of Pope, the poetic authority of the eighteenth century, it is joined, for instance, with *bound, found, ground*. Yet this same pronunciation was unequivocally condemned by Walker at the end of the same century. "To *wound*," he writes, "is sometimes pronounced so as to rhyme with *found;* but this is directly contrary to the best usage."

This same uncertainty in the pronunciation of words in consequence of the uncertainty of the pronunciation of the signs employed to represent it may be further exemplified in the case of the noun *route*. Unlike *wound*, which is a pure native word, this is of French extraction. Following the analogy of most of the words so derived, it ought to have the second sound given here to the digraph. Yet it not unfrequently receives that of the first. Thus Walker graciously tells us that it is often pro-

154

nounced so as to ryme with *doubt* "by respectable speakers." A far more interesting case is
that of *pour*. The majority of eighteenth century orthoepists—Johnston, Kenrick, Perry,
Smith, and Walker—pronounced the word so
as to ryme with *power*. Spenser so employed
it. So did Pope, more than a century later.
In the only two instances he uses the word in
his regular poetry at the end of a line it has this
sound. In his *Messiah* occurs the following
couplet:

Ye Heavens! from high the dewy nectar pour:
And in soft silence shed the kindly shower.

Walker, indeed, declared unreservedly that the
best pronunciation of it is "that similar to
power." Nares alone among eighteenth century
orthoepists seems to have upheld what is now
the customary pronunciation; yet even here the
authority of some of the greatest of modern
poets has been occasionally cast in favor of the
once accepted sound. In his poem of *The
Poet's Mind*, Tennyson, for instance, writes:

Holy water will I pour
Into every spicy flower.

The digraph is far from being limited to
the sounds heard respectively in *thou* and *you*.

Another one is that of long *o*, found, for illustration, in *dough, soul, mould.* There is still another sound—that of the so-called "broad *a*"—
which is heard in *brought, ought,* and *wrought.*
A fifth sound represented is that of the regular
short *u* seen in *would, could,* and *should.* In
cough and *trough*, as pronounced by many, there
is a sixth sound represented. In the course of
its travels through the vowel sounds the sign
reaches that which we commonly call "short
u." There is no small number of words in
which this pronunciation of it appears. *Country,
journey, trouble, flourish* may be given as examples. *Ou*, in truth, has a remarkable record,
not so much by the number of sounds it represents—in this it is approached by two or three
other digraphs—but by the comparative largeness of the body of words in which several of
these different sounds appear. In the latter
respect, but not at all in the former, is it rivalled
by the analogous *ow.* This, common as it is,
has but two sounds. The first and most frequent is that heard in *brown, down,* and *vowel;*
the second is the long *o* sound heard in such
words as *blow, grow,* and *below.*

We now reach the digraphs of which the
vowel *u* is the first letter. In a large number of
words this has, if pronounced, the sound of *w.*

Especially is this true of syllables upon which no accent falls, or at most a secondary accent. Nothing of this characteristic is seen in the case of *uy*—in which the diphthongal sound of *i* is heard in the two words *buy* and *guy*—but it is noticeable in the case of the first four vowels. We can see it illustrated by the *ua* of *assuage*, *persuade*, *language;* by the *ue* of *conquest*, *request*, and *desuetude;* by the *ui* of *anguish*, *languish*, *cuirass;* and by the *uo* of *quote*, *quota*, *quorum.* In this last case the *u* strictly belongs with *q.* Of *ua*, the first of these digraphs, all that needs to be said is that in certain words, such as *guard* and *guardian*, the *u* is not pronounced at all. The same statement can be made of *ue* in *guess*, *guest*, *guerdon.* It is as useless as it is silent. A plea has been put forth in justification of its existence on the theory that it acts as a sort of servile instrument to protect the hard sound of *g.* If this digraph were invariably so employed, it may be conceded that there would be some sense in its existence. But he who expects to find either sense or consistency in English orthography has strayed beyond the limits of justifiable ignorance. There is a large number of instances in which the consonant *g* continues to exhibit its hard sound when followed directly by *e. Get* and *geese*

and *gewgaw* and *eager* and *anger* are a few of the
words which could be adduced to show that
there has never been felt any necessity of the
presence of a protecting *u* to indicate this
pronunciation.

When at the end of a word the digraph *ue* has
often the sound of long *u*, as in *blue*, *pursue*,
true, and *rue*. But no small number of instances occur in which it is entirely silent.
This is especially noticeable in words derived
from the Greek which have the final syllables
logue or *gogue*. *Catalogue*, *prologue*, *dialogue*,
demagogue, *pedagogue*, and *synagogue* will serve
as examples. But the list of words in which
this digraph is silent is far from being confined
to those with these two terminations. *Antique*,
oblique, *intrigue*, *colleague*, *fatigue*, *rogue*, and
plague will testify to the uselessness of it as
far as pronunciation is concerned, unless it be
maintained that it justifies its existence by indicating that the preceding vowel has a long
sound. If this be true, it ought not to appear
when the vowel is short. One sees so much of
the results of freak and wantonness in our spelling that it is permissible to cherish the fancy
that any intelligent principle has been some-
time somewhere at work in it, and that a feeling
of this kind was the unconscious motive that

led to the adoption of *packet* in place of *pacquet* and of *lackey* for *lacquey;* at any rate, of *risk* for the once prevalent *risque* and of *check* for *cheque*. But no such reason can be assigned for the *ue* of *tongue*. Its original was *tunge*. The final *e* ceased to be pronounced, and in course of time to be printed. The insertion of a *u* in the ending, after the fashion of the French *langue*, was an act of combined ignorance and folly.

The digraph *ui* follows in general the course of *ue*. As in the case of the latter the *u* was found unneeded in *guess* and *guest*, so it is equally unnecessary in *guide* and *guile*. Here again a not dissimilar sort of defence for it has been set up. Its retention, we are told, is desirable in order to indicate the diphthongal sound of *i* in these words. The argument is as futile as in the case of the preceding digraph. It illustrates forcibly the capabilities of our spelling in the way of confusing pronunciation that the same combination which is responsible for "long *i*" in *guide* and *guile* and *disguise* is equally responsible for the short *i* of *guilt*, *guinea*, and *build*. With the statement that *ui* has still another sound in such words as *fruit*, *bruise*, and *recruit*, we leave the consideration of the vowels and vowel sounds. But after the survey of the subject which has just been made, no one is likely to pretend that the pronunciation he hears of any one of these in a strange word will furnish him the least surety that he will be able to reproduce its authorized form in writing.

v

THE CONSONANTS

So much for the vowels. When we come to the consonants we are approaching much more solid phonetic ground. In a general way, they have remained faithful to the sounds they were created to indicate. Not but that here also there is need of reform. This will be made sufficiently manifest when details are given in the case of individual letters. But the disorganization of the consonant - system is slight compared with that of the vowel-system. There is, indeed, a fundamental difference between the two. With the vowels conformity to any phonetic law whatever is the exception and not the rule. With the consonants the reverse is the case. Fortunate it is for the English-speaking race that such is the fact. Were it otherwise, were there with the consonants the same degree of irregularity which exists with the vowels, the same degree of variableness in the representation of sounds, the same widely

160

prevalent indifference to analogy, knowledge of English spelling would not be delayed, as it is now, for no more than two or three years beyond the normal time of its acquisition; it would be the work of a lifetime. Mastery of it, under existing conditions never fully gained by some, would in such circumstances never be acquired by anybody who learned anything else.

There is one pervading characteristic of the consonants which differentiates their position in the orthography from that of the vowels. Wherever they appear they have ordinarily the pronunciation which is theirs by right. Ordinarily, not invariably. There are exceptions that demand full discussion. Still, the usual way in which consonants vary from the phonetic standard is not by being pronounced differently but by not being pronounced at all. In some instances the useless letter represents the derivation; in others it defies it. They have been retained in the spelling, though never pronounced, either because they are found in the primitive from which they came; or they have been introduced into it under the influence of a false analogy, or as a consequence of a false derivation. In any reform of the orthography it may not be desirable in some cases to drop— at all events at the outset—these now silent

letters. It assuredly would not be so wherever
the tendency manifests itself to resume them in
pronunciation.

There are four of the consonants which practically do not vary from phonetic law. They
are never silent; they always indicate the
precise pronunciation which they purport to
indicate. In the case of two of them there is in
each a single instance in which the rule does not
hold good. In the preposition *of*, *f* has the
sound of *v*. In the matter of inflection the
temptation to retain this letter in spite of the
change of sound has been successfully resisted.
So we very properly say *calves* and *wolves* instead of *calfs* and *wolfs*, though this course exhibits what some must feel to be a scandalous
tendency toward phonetic spelling. The other
letter is *m*. The only exception to its regular
pronunciation is found in the word sometimes
spelled *comptroller*. Here it has the sound of
n. But this has already been pointed out as a
well-known spurious form based upon a spurious
derivation. Its first syllable was supposed to
come from the French *compter* and not from its
real original, the Latin *contra*. The affection
for this corrupt form now felt by some is in
curious contrast with the attitude taken toward
count both as a verb and a noun. These words

were once often spelled like the corresponding
French *compte* and *compter*. There was justification for this. They all came from the remote Latin original *computare*, in which the *p*
is found. Naturally this particular spelling was
especially prevalent in the sixteenth century,
when derivation ran rampant in the orthography; but the practice extended much later. Had
compt continued in use and fastened itself upon
the language, we can imagine, but we cannot
adequately express, the indignation that would
now be felt by many worthy people at the proposal of any reformer to substitute for it *count*,
and the picture of ruin to the speech that would
be drawn as a result of such a wanton defiance
of the derivation.

Let us now consider the unpronounced consonants. In the remote past such letters when
no longer wanted were regularly dropped. Now
they are as regularly retained. They are retained not because they are needed, but because
they have become familiar to the eye. They
naturally fall into three classes, according as
they appear at the beginning, at the end, or in
the middle of a word. To the first class belong
g and *k* when followed by *n; w* followed by *ho* or
by *r;* and the aspirate *h*. The failure to pronounce this last in certain words is too well

163

known to need here more than a reference. Elsewhere, too, I have given an account of the gradual resumption of the sound of this letter.[1] There are about half a dozen words in which an initial *g* is silent. Of these *gnaw* and *gnat* may be taken as examples. There are more than double this number in which an initial *k* before the same letter *n* is not heard. These are adequately represented, with the different vowels following, by *knave, knee, knife, know,* and *knuckle.* Still more frequently unsounded is an initial *w.* There are fully two dozen and a half of words in which this letter is not pronounced. The class finds satisfactory exemplification in *who, whole, wrap, wrest, wrist, wrong,* and *wry.* In making up these numbers it must be kept in mind that neither derivatives nor compounds are taken into account. Were such to be included, the list would be largely swelled.

In the cases just considered a letter once sounded has disappeared from the spoken tongue. The fact of its disappearance from pronunciation has not, however, induced men, as was once the practice, to discard it from the written tongue. But there are instances in which the initial consonant has never been heard

[1] *Standard of Pronunciation in English,* pp. 191-202.

at all in the utterance of any speakers. The words to which they belong are of foreign origin. They come to us with the foreign spelling. In many cases, or rather in most, they are from the Greek. The conspicuous examples are the *c* of *czar*, now frequently spelled *tsar* with the *t* sounded, the *p* of *psalm* and *pseudo* and of several compounds in which the *psi* of the Hellenic alphabet furnishes the initial letter. The same uselessness extends to *ph*—seen, for illustration, in the form *phthisic*—and to the *p* of words of Greek origin beginning with *pt*. It may be remarked in passing that there is a curious blunder in the spelling of the name of the bird called the *ptarmigan*. This is a pure Celtic word, which begins with *t*. To it a *p* was prefixed, possibly because it was supposed to be of Greek origin.

The final consonants which are retained in the spelling but are not heard in the pronunciation are *b*, *n*, *h*, *t*, *w*, and *x*. The words possessing them may be divided into two classes. In one the useless letter has a sort of claim to existence. It was there originally. Let us begin with the unpronounced final *b*. The native words ending in it are *climb*, *comb*, *dumb*, and *lamb*. They are common to the various Teutonic languages. In all of these they ter-

minated originally with this consonant. To
the list may be added *plumb*, 'perpendicular,'
coming remotely from the Latin *plumbum*,
'lead.' The spelling of these words underwent
the usual variations common before a fixed orthography had fastened itself upon the speech.
Naturally the unpronounced *b* was not unfrequently dropped. This was especially true of
climb and *dumb*. Take as an illustration Spenser's line, where he speaks of a castle-wall,

That was so high as foe might not it clime.[1]

But after the reign of Elizabeth the useless letter gradually but firmly fixed its hold upon the
spelling in the case of all these words. In this
respect English has had a different development
from that of other Teutonic tongues. Take
modern German, for instance. For the word
corresponding to *climb* it has replaced the original *chlimban* by *klimmen*; for *chamb*, 'comb,'
it has substituted *kamm;* for *dumb* in Old High
German *tumb*, it has *dumm;* for *lamb*, in Old
High German *lamb*, it has *lamm*. The dropping of the final *b* seems to have wrought no
observable harm to the language nor occasioned

[1] *Faerie Queene*, Book II, canto ix, st. 21.

any grief—at all events, any present grief—to its users.

Still, it may be maintained in justification of the present spelling of these words that they are entitled to the final *b* on the ground of derivation. But no such plea can be put up in the case of those now to be considered. These are *crumb*, *limb*, *numb*, and *thumb*. In all of these the last letter is not only useless, but according to the term one chooses to employ, it is either a blunder or a corruption. It did not exist in the original. In truth, this unnecessary consonant threatened at one time to fasten itself also upon the name of the fruit called the *plum*. Especially was this noticeable in the best literature of the eighteenth century. An attack of common sense, to which the users of our orthography have been occasionally liable, prevented this particular word from carrying about the burden of the unpronounced *b*. In the case of most of the others it was not until the sixteenth century that the practice began of appending the unauthorized and unneeded letter. It took something of a struggle to foist it upon these words; but not so much, indeed, as will be required to loose the hold it has now gained over the hearts of thousands.

There are a few words, almost all of Latin

derivation, in which a final *n* appears unsounded. *Kiln* is perhaps the only one of English extraction in which this peculiarity appears. In the case of most of them the retention of the letter may be defended—at least it may be palliated—on the ground that in the derivatives its pronunciation is resumed. In *autumn, column, condemn, hymn*, and *limn* the *n* is silent, but it gives distinct evidence of its existence in words like *autumnal, columnar, condemnation, hymnal, limner*, and *solemnity*. In fact, this resumption of the sound has at times been made to appear in other parts of the verbs containing this silent letter. Especially has this been true of *hymning* and *limning*, the participles of *hymn* and *limn*. It was a practice which much grieved certain of the earlier orthoepists. They took the ground that analogy forbade any sound not belonging to the principal verb itself to be heard in any of its parts. The observation is only noticeable for its revelation of the fact that it should enter into the head of any advocate of the existing orthography to set up analogy as a convincing reason for pronouncing any English word in a particular way.

Three of these final unpronounced letters do not need protracted consideration. In the digraph *ow*, ending such words as *low*, *flow*, and *sow*, the *w* serves no particular use. According to some it justifies its existence by indicating the quality of the preceding vowel. Its value in this respect may be estimated by comparing the pronunciation of *bow*, a missile weapon for discharging an arrow, with *bow*, an inclination of the head, or *bow*, the fore-end of a boat. The next letter *t*, when a final consonant, is invariably heard, save in some imperfectly naturalized words. Of these *eclat* and *billet-doux* may be taken as examples. In England, however—not in the United States—there is a single and singular survival of the original French pronunciation in the case of a word received into full citizenship. This is the noun *trait*, which came into the language in the eighteenth century. Naturally its final letter was at first not sounded. The tendency so to do, however, soon showed itself. Lexicographers authorized it, indeed favored it; but for some inexplicable reason Englishmen have never taken kindly to the complete naturalization of the word. "The *t*," said Walker, at the end of the eighteenth century, "begins to be pronounced." Had he been living at the end of the nineteenth, he would have been justified in saying precisely the same thing as regards England. It was

169

beginning then; it is beginning now; but it is only beginning.

A final *h* is not pronounced when preceded by a vowel; when preceded by the consonant *g* it forms a digraph which will be considered later. There are fewer than a dozen words of the former class in which it appears. Among these are the interjections, *ah, eh,* and *oh.* Here again, as in the case of *w,* the existence of the letter is defended on the ground that it indicates the quality of the preceding vowel. Yet for this purpose it can hardly be deemed a necessity. We use it in the case of *ah;* but we get along very well without it in the case of *ha.* This, too, was formerly sometimes spelled *hah.* *Oh,* likewise, was once widely found in the very instances and the very senses where we now use the single letter *O.* In two other words, *Messiah* and *hallelujah,* the *h* may be retained because of the sacredness of associations which have gathered about them. Yet the former word was itself a sixteenth-century alteration of the previous *Messias.*

The unpronounced final *k* belongs strictly to the class of double letters of which it is not my purpose to treat. It invariably follows *c,* and is really nothing but a duplicate of it. Still, as the sign is a different representation of the same sound, it may be well to bestow upon it a brief attention. At the end of the eighteenth and the beginning of the nineteenth century it was dropped, after a warm contest, from words of Latin derivation. But the reform did not extend to those of native origin. In many cases a *k* has been added to words which originally ended in *c*. Especially was this true of monosyllables. Thus the earliest form of *back* was *bæc*, of *sack* was *sac*, of *sick* was *seoc*. This was the case not only with a good many monosyllables to which a *k* is now appended, but to a certain extent with dissyllables also. The fact is best exemplified in the words which have the ending *ock*. This sometimes represents the early English diminutive *uc*, which became later *oc* or *ok*. From the point of view of derivation the modern spelling is distinctly improper. Thus, for illustration, *bullock*, *haddock*, *hassock*, *hillock*, and *mattock* were in their earliest known forms *bulluc*, *haddoc*, *hassuc*, *hilloc*, and *mattuc*. Several words not of native origin have also adopted this ending. *Hammock*, from the Spanish *hamaca*, itself of Carib origin, has conformed to it. It has supplied itself with a final *k*. During the last century *havoc* managed to get rid of this consonant, with which it had been encumbered, without excit-

171

ing any special remark. But now that the use-lessness of a letter has become to many one of the chief recommendations of the spelling, the dropping of an unnecessary *k* from any of the other words of this class would bring unspeakable anguish to thousands.

There are more consonants which are unpronounced in the middle of words than at the beginning or the end. They are *b*, *c*, *l*, *g*, *h*, *p*, *s*, *t*, *w*, and *z*. In the case of some of them—the two last, for instance—the words in which the unpronounced letter appears are very few. In *rendezvous z* is not sounded. It is the only instance in which this consonant is not heard, and this is due to the fact that it is not heard in its French original. Again, it is only in *answer*, *sword*, and *two* that the medial *w* is silent. Unpronounced consonants are more frequent in the case of the other letters, but, after all, they are not numerous in themselves. Still, their presence has its usual effect. In every instance it raises a stumbling-block in the way of the proper pronunciation. Furthermore, it has in some cases either hidden the right derivation entirely or given a wrong idea of it.

Take the example of the medial *b* in *debt* and *doubt*. These words, coming originally from the French, were introduced into the language

with the spelling, *dette, det,* and *doute, dout.* So
for a long time they were spelled. Deference
to the remote Latin original, which sprang up
with the revival of learning, introduced the unauthorized *b* into the world. It has already
been pointed out that this has given an opportunity, which has been fully improved, for
the devotees of derivation to exhibit their usual
inconsistency. When the presence of unpronounced letters in the case of other words presents an obstacle to correct pronunciation, then
its retention is insisted upon as essential to our
knowledge of its immediate origin, to the purity
of the language itself, and to the happiness of
those speaking it. But no advocate of the
existing orthography could be induced to part
with the *b* of *debt* and *doubt,* though its presence
comes into direct conflict with the views he is
championing in the case of other words. At
times attempts were apparently made to pronounce the inserted *b.* In the full Latinized
form *debit,* which was early in use, there was no
difficulty. Indeed, it was a necessity. Not so
in the form *debt.* Yet it is evident from *Love's
Labour's Lost* that there were men who sought
to accomplish this feat. It is difficult to ascertain whether speaker or hearer suffered more in
consequence of this effort. If unsuccessful, it

was the speaker; if successful, the pain was transferred to the hearer.

One curious blunder has been foisted upon our spelling by the desire of men to go back to the Latin original of these words instead of contenting themselves with the immediate French one. The insertion of *b* is bad enough in *redoubted* and *redoubtable*. These came to us from the latter tongue, and at first appeared in English in the forms *redouted* and *redoutable*. Later the classical influence made itself felt and the *b* was inserted. Palliation for it could be pleaded on the ground that the letter belonged to the remote original. But no defence of this sort could be of avail in the case of the word denoting the military outwork called a *redoubt*. This has not the slightest connection either in sense or origin with the two adjectives just specified. It comes directly from the French *redout* and remotely from the Latin *reductus*, 'withdrawn,' 'retired,' which received at a later period the meaning of 'a place of refuge.' But it was ignorantly supposed that it came from the same source as the verb *redoubt* and its past participle *redoubted*. So from the beginning of the introduction of the word into the language, in the early part of the seventeenth century, an unauthorized *b* was made part of it.

It is now dear to the hearts of millions. What the blundering of one age perpetrated the superstition of succeeding ages has invested with peculiar sanctity.

The cases in which *c* follows *s* present several choice examples of the vagaries which make English orthography a wonder to those who study its history, and a perpetual joy and boast to those who in this matter succeed in keeping the purity of their ignorance from being defiled by the slightest stain of knowledge. In the words *scene*, *scepter*, and *sciatica*, coming directly or remotely from the Greek, the letter represents an original *k*. So, useless as it is, its retention may be defended on the ground that if it be not the same letter, it ought to be, since it has the same value. The similar apology of respect for derivation may be urged for the unpronounced *c* of *science*, *scintilla*, and *sciolist*. But in the case of *scent*, *scion*, *scimitar*, *scissors*, and *scythe*, no such plea can be made. In the instance of all these there is not the slightest justification for the unnecessary *c*. *Scent* comes from the Latin *sent-ire*, 'to perceive.' Until the seventeenth century it was regularly spelled *sent*. *Scythe*, from the Anglo-Saxon *sîthe*, once frequently and now occasionally has its strictly correct etymological form. *Scion* is from the old French *sion*. *Scimitar* and *scissors* have had a wide variety of spellings during the course of their history. English orthography has exhibited, as is not unusual, a perverse preference for the ones which depart furthest from the pronunciation.

The instances where *g* is silent within a word are those in which it is found preceding *m* or *n*. Its presence it owes, in most instances, to derivation. Examples of it can be found in a number of words of Greek extraction, of which *paradigm*, *diaphragm*, and *phlegm* may be given. With a following *n* it can be represented by *campaign*, *feign*, *sign*, and *impugn*. As has been the case with the final *n* of certain words, so also the pronunciation of the *g* is resumed in the derivatives. That may be deemed by some a justification for its retention in the primitive—at least, for the time being. With *sign* we have *signify*, with *malign* we have *malignity*, with *phlegm* we have *phlegmatic*. But the *g* is a particularly ridiculous intruder in the words *foreign* and *sovereign*. The former is from the Old French *forein*, which itself comes from the popular Latin *foraneus*, and this in turn comes from the classical Latin *foras*, 'out of doors.' *Sovereign* is a spelling just as bad. It comes from the Old French *sovrain*, the Low

Latin *superanus*, 'supreme,' which was formed
upon the preposition *super*, 'above.' The insertion of a *g* was a blunder for which our race has
the sole responsibility.

There are two kinds of words in which *h* is
silent following an initial letter. This is invariably true of words of Greek extraction beginning with *rh*. *Rhetoric, rheumatic*, and *rhu-
barb* may serve as specimens. In these, as in
those like them, the *h* was wanting in Old French.
Consequently, it was at first wanting in English
also. But the deference to derivation which
prevailed among the classically educated after
the revival of learning, raised havoc here with
the spelling as it did in so many other instances.
The unpronounced *h* was inserted into all these
words. This began in the sixteenth century.
It gradually established itself firmly in the
orthography. There it has remained ever since,
though no one pretends that it serves any purpose save that of indicating to the few, who
do not need to be informed, that the aspirate
existed in the original from which these words
were derived. But even this pitiable reason
cannot be pleaded in the case of the noticeable
words in which *h* follows an initial *g*. These
are *ghastly* and *aghast, ghost*, and *gherkin*. In
not one of them, except the last, did *h* ap-

pear till many hundred years after the words had been in existence. To not one of them does the useless letter belong by right. Indeed, it was apparently not till the nineteenth century that it was foisted into *gherkin* as the regular spelling, though it had cropped up before. There would be just as much sense in spelling *German* as *Gherman*, and *goat* as *ghoat*, as there is in the intrusion of the *h* into the words just mentioned. This is equally true of *anchor*.

There is, however, one further peculiarity about this letter. In the spelling of certain words it follows *w*, in the pronunciation of them it precedes it. But the fashion of suppressing the sound of the aspirate in the combination *wh* is very characteristic of the speech of England, at least of some parts of it. The prevalence of this sort of pronunciation which makes no distinction, for example, between *where* and *wear*, between *Whig* and *wig*, between *while* and *wile*, was a subject of great, and it may be added, of justifiable grief to the earlier orthoepists. Walker complained bitterly of the extent of its use in London. He was anxious that men should "avoid this feeble Cockney pronunciation which is so disagreeable to a correct ear." Fortunately for the speech this suppression of the aspirate has not extended much beyond the southern half of England. In America it rarely takes place. There is, therefore, every likelihood of this pronunciation being eventually crushed, not so much because of its own inherent viciousness as by the mere weight of numbers.

There is a limited body of words in which *l* and *p* are silent. The former letter in such cases as *balm* and *calm*, for instance, may perhaps have been effective in preserving the sound of the preceding vowel. The most signal example of its appearance, where it has no justification for its existence, is in the word *could*. This takes the place of the earlier and more correct *coude, coud*. The *l* was introduced by a false analogy with *would* and *should*. These two last words, it may be added, at times dropped this letter, to which etymologically they were entitled, out of deference to the pronunciation, just as *could*, though not entitled to it, assumed it in defiance of the pronunciation.

The most noticeable instances in which *p* is not pronounced are when it follows *m* and is itself followed by *t*. *Empty, tempt, prompt*, and *sumptuous* will supply a sufficient number of illustrations. In most of these cases the letter still appears because it was in the original. In *empty*, however, it is a later insertion. There

179

are two or three sporadic instances in which a *p* is present but fails to be called upon for duty. Such are *raspberry* and *receipt*. In the first of these two *rasberry* seems to have been for a long time the preferred spelling. Unless there is a prospect that the sound of the letter will be resumed in the pronunciation, there is no apparent reason why we should not go back to the once more common form. But *receipt*, with the allied *conceit* and *deceit*, furnishes as good an illustration as can well be offered of the vagaries of English orthography, and of the system which has prevailed in and the sense which has presided over its development. These three words all come remotely from the three closely allied participial forms *receptus*, *conceptus*, and *deceptus*. The earlier most common spelling of the first was *receit* or *receyt*. While the form with the inserted *p* existed previously, it was not till the Elizabethan period that it began to be much in evidence. Furthermore, it was not till the latter part of the seventeenth century that the unnecessary letter established itself in the unfortunate word. *Conceit* and *deceit* went through what was in many respects the same experience. The forms *conceipt* and *deceipt* were found not unfrequently. But in them the *p* failed to maintain itself.

So words from a common Latin root have developed two different ways of spelling, with not the slightest reason in the nature of things why any distinction whatever should be made between them.

The silence of *s* in some few words, such as *isle*, *aisle*, and *island*, has already been mentioned. In *viscount* it is also suppressed, doubtless in deference to the French original. But in the middle of words *t* is far more frequently left unpronounced than *s*. This is especially noticeable when it is followed by *le* on the one hand, as can be seen in *castle*, *wrestle*, *thistle*, *ostler*, and *rustle;* on the other hand, when followed by *en*, as in *fasten*, *hasten*, *listen*, and *moisten*. There are a few other words besides those with these endings in which it is silent. Such are *Christmas*, *chestnut*, *mortgage*, *bankruptcy*. That it should not be heard in words of French origin like *billet-doux* and *hautbois* is not hard to understand; they have never been fully naturalized.

This exhausts the list of simple consonants that are found in the written language, but are not heard in the spoken. There remains, however, a digraph which is encountered too frequently not to receive brief mention. This is *gh*, both at the end and in the middle of words. In these positions it once stood for something.

It had, therefore, originally a right to the place in which it now appears. But the guttural sound it indicated disappeared long ago from the usage of all of us. Even the knowledge that it had ever existed has disappeared from the memory of most of us, if it was ever found there. Accordingly it serves now no other purpose than to act as a sort of tombstone to mark the place where lie the unsightly remains of a dead and forgotten pronunciation. The useless digraph is still seen at the end of numerous words of which *weigh*, *high*, and *dough* may be taken as examples. Again an unpronounced medial *gh* is seen in *neighbor* and a large number of words ending in *ght*, such as *caught*, *height*, *fight*, and *thought*. In many of these words the digraph was frequently dropped in those earlier days when there was a perverse propensity to make the spelling show some respect to the pronunciation. *High*, for instance, often appeared in the forms *hye*, *hy; nigh* in the forms *nye*, *ny*. This is now all changed. The disposition to pander to any sneaking desire to bring about a scandalous conformity between orthography and orthoepy is steadily frowned upon by those who have been good enough to take upon their shoulders the burden of preserving what they are pleased to call the purity of the English language.

This survey of the subject, brief as it is, brings out distinctly the superiority of the consonant system over the vowel, in the matter of unpronounced letters. Far from perfect as is the former, it shines by contrast with the latter. The useless consonant appears in but a few words, where the useless vowel appears in scores. But when we pass on to the cases in which the sign is represented by any but its legitimate sound, the contrast between the two classes of letters becomes far more noticeable. It is the superiority in this particular which alone makes our present spelling endurable. Most of the consonants, if pronounced at all, have in all cases one and the same sound. Any possible acquisition of the speech in the term of a man's natural life has depended upon the fact that these members of the alphabet are in general really phonetic. Their faithfulness to their legitimate sounds stands in sharpest contrast to the almost hopeless disorganization which has overtaken the vowels. In the case of some of the consonants there is never any variation from their proper pronunciation. In the case of others the exceptions to the regular practice are purely sporadic. The *p* of *cupboard*, for instance, has the sound of *b*, the *j* of *hallelujah* has the sound of *y*. Even these exceptions which have prevailed in the past there has been a tendency to reduce, owing to the operation of agencies of which there will be occasion to speak later.

This last statement needs modification in the case of one letter. In modern times there has been a tendency to represent the sound of *t* in the preterite and past participle by *d*, or, rather, *ed*. As compared with the usage of the past, this practice has made a good deal of headway. It is the substitution of a formal regularity of spelling which appeals to the eye over its proper use to indicate the sound to the ear. We have not yet got so far as to write *sleeped* for *slept* or *feeled* for *felt*, but we have frequently *dwelled* for *dwelt* and *builded* for *built*. This is all proper enough if the *d* sound is given to the ending by pronouncing the word, as is often done, as a dissylable. But no reason can be pleaded for it if *t* is heard as the termination. In this matter we are far behind our fathers.

Take the usage of Spenser, as illustrated on this point in the first canto of the first book of the *Faerie Queene*. This contains about five hundred lines. In every case whenever a preterite or past participle has the sound of *t*, it is spelled with *t*. In this one canto—and it fairly represents all the others—can be found the preterites *advaunst, approcht, chaunst, en-haunst, forst, glaunst, grypt, knockt, lept, lookt, nurst, pusht, y-rockt, stopt*, and *tost*. Along with these are to be seen as past participles *accurst, enforst, mixt, past, promist, stretcht, vanquisht*, and *wrapt*. Now, to a certain extent this is an unfair illustration. No one can read the *Faerie Queene* without becoming aware that Spenser was a good deal of a spelling reformer. Necessarily, he was largely dominated by the ignoble idea that orthography should have a close connection with the pronunciation. Still, though in certain particulars he took very advanced ground, he only practiced on a large scale what on a small scale was followed by very many of his contemporaries and immediate successors.

We pass on now to the consideration of the six sounds for which the alphabet has no special sign whatever. Two of them are the surd and sonant sounds, already considered, for which the digraph *th* has become the common representative. It may be right to add that this same digraph is also equivalent in a few cases to the simple *t*, as in *thyme* and *Thames*. The four other sounds can be recognized perhaps most easily in the *ch* of *church*, the *ng* of *bring*, the *sh* of *ship*, and the *s* of *pleasure*. But here,

185

as elsewhere in our orthography, reigns the usual lawlessness. The signs here given represent other sounds than those just specified. Take the case of *ng*. Any one can detect at once the difference in the pronunciation of this digraph by contrasting it as heard in *singer* and as heard in *finger*. Nor has *ch* been limited to the sound indicated in *chair*, *cheer*, *child*, *choose*, and *churn*. It has another, perhaps more frequently denoted by *sh* in the beginning, middle, and end of words, as, for illustration, in *chaise*, *machine*, and *bench*. It has likewise the sound of *k* in many words, especially in those of Greek origin, such as *character*, *mechanic*, *monarch*. The uncertainty caused by this variety of pronunciation is particularly noticeable in words in which *arch* appears as the initial syllable. In *archangel*, for instance, *ch* has one pronunciation, in *archbishop* it has another. The difference between the two must therefore be painfully learned. There is, furthermore, the sporadic example of *choir*, in which *ch* has the sound of *kw*, ordinarily represented by *qu*. But *choir* was a late seventeenth-century importation into the language. Though to some extent it has replaced the original form *quire*, it has invariably retained the pronunciation of that word.

Finally, there are the two sounds specified

186

above, as denoted by the *s* of *pleasure* and the *sh* of *ship*. The former has a respectable number of signs to indicate it. Besides the *s* found in such words as *measure, usury, enclosure,* it is represented by *si,* as seen in *decision, evasion, occasion;* by *z,* as in *azure, razure, seizure;* by *zi,* as in *glazier, grazier, vizier.* It is, however, the second of these sounds that has the greatest variety of signs to denote it. In this respect it rivals many of the vowels or vowel combinations, and surpasses some of them. It is heard in the *ce* of *ocean,* and in particular in no small number of words mainly scientific, with the ending *aceous,* such as *cretaceous* and *cetaceous;* in the *ci* of words like *social, gracious, suspicion;* in the *s* of *sure, sugar, censure, nauseate;* in the *t* of *satiate, expatiate, substantiate;* in the *ti* of *martial, patient, nation,* and the vast number of words which have the termination *tion;* in *xi* in *anxious, obnoxious, complexion;* in *sci* in *conscience, prescience;* in *si,* as seen in no small number of words, such as *mansion, vision, explosion.* Finally, to illustrate the confusion which in the case of these signs has been still further confounded, we may instance the *ci* of *social* with the pronunciation just indicated, and the *ci* of the related word *society* with a pronunciation entirely different. A precisely similar observa-

187

tion could be made of *ti* in the case of the words *satiate* and *satiety*.

Enough has certainly now been said to put beyond question the fact of the irrepressible conflict which goes on in our language between orthography and orthoepy, and to make clear its nature. The treatment of the subject has, indeed, been far from complete. Nothing whatever has been said on the large subject of the representation of sounds in the unaccented syllables. No account has been given of the usage of some of the letters or combinations of letters. In particular, in the matter of doubling the letters both in accented and unaccented syllables, contradictions and incongruities abound with us on a scale which ought to bring peculiar happiness to those devotees of the present orthography who believe that the worse a language is spelled the more distinctly it is to its credit. Still, of this characteristic there has been no consideration. Furthermore, page after page could have been taken up with illustrative examples of the anarchy of all sorts which reigns in every nook and corner of our spelling. We write, for instance, *knowledge* with a *d;* but the place with the same terminating syllable where we go presumably to acquire it, which we call a *college*, we are careful to write without a *d*.

SPELLING REFORM

In the past one finds at times the forms *knowl-ege* and *colledge*. It is nothing but an accident of usage that we are not employing them now instead of the ones we have adopted.

It would be easy to go on multiplying examples of these inconsistencies. But though all that could be said is far from having been said, surely enough has been given to prove beyond possibility of denial the existence of the chaotic condition which prevails. Furthermore, while the subject has been by no means exhausted, the same statement cannot safely be made of the patience of the reader, to say nothing of that of the writer. If any one of the former body finds it tedious to wade through the account of the situation which has been given in the preceding pages, let him bear in mind how much more tedious it was for the author to prepare it. If he finds it exceedingly tedious, let him take to himself a sort of consolation in the reflection of how easily it could have been made even more so. Instead, therefore, of complaining of the abundance of minute detail which I have supplied, he ought to be thankful to me for keeping back so much of it as I have done. Moreover, as Heine pointed out long ago, the reader has at his command a resource to which he can always betake himself when his powers of endurance give out. He can skip. This is a blessed privilege denied to the writer.

Incomplete, however, as has been the survey of the subject, it has been sufficient to give a fairly satisfactory idea of the way in which the orthography represents, or rather misrepresents, the pronunciation. It makes manifest beyond dispute the truth of the intimation conveyed at the outset that the form of a particular word is often, with us, little more than a fortuitous concourse of unrelated letters in which neither they nor the combinations into which they enter can be relied upon to indicate any particular sound. In addition, hundreds of those which appear in the spelling have no office in the pronunciation. Genuine derivation has led to the retention of some, spurious derivation to the introduction of others. There are, consequently, few of the common words of our language which cannot be spelled with perfect propriety in different ways, sometimes in half a dozen different ways, if the analogy be followed of words similarly formed and pronounced. Our orthography is, therefore, often a matter of contention and always a matter of study. Knowledge of the accepted form of words must be gained in each case independently, for there exists no general principle, the observance of

which will guide the learner to a correct conclusion.

As an inevitable result, the acquisition of
spelling never calls into exercise, with us, the
reasoning faculties. On the contrary, its direct
effect is to keep them in abeyance. The ability
to spell properly is an intellectual act only to the
extent that attention and recollection are intellectual acts. It can and not unfrequently
does characterize persons who are very far from
being gifted with much mental power. All
who attain proficiency in it are compelled to
spend time which, under proper conditions, could
have been far more profitably employed. There
are men who do not attain it at an early age, and
some even who never attain it at all. Moore, for
illustration, speaking of Byron, tells us that
spelling was "a very late accomplishment with
him." [1] The case of William Morris was far
worse. This poet never learned to spell at all.
The fact is recorded by his biographer. In
speaking of the beauty of his handwriting, he
had to admit the failure of his orthography to
reach the standard set by it. "The subsidiary
art of spelling," he writes, "was always one in
which he was liable to make curious lapses. 'I

---

[1] *Moore's Diary*, vol. v, p. 249.

remember,' the poet once said, 'being taught to spell and standing on a chair with my shoes off because I made so many mistakes.' In later years several sheets of *The Life and Death of Jason* had to be cancelled and reprinted because of a mistake in the spelling of a perfectly common English word; a word, indeed, so common that the printer's reader had left it as it was in the manuscript, thinking that Morris' spelling must be an intentional peculiarity." [1]

The ignorance which exists in regard to the orthographic situation is bad enough; but the superstition which has been born of it is still worse. It is assumed to have come down to us pure and perfect from a remote past. Hence, it must be religiously preserved in all its assumed sacredness and genuine uncouthness. Even improvements which could be made with little difficulty, which would have no other result than bringing about with the least possible friction uniformity in certain classes of words —these slight alterations are assailed with almost as much earnestness and virulence as would be encountered by sweeping changes designed to make the spelling really phonetic.

As men are more apt to be interested in particu-

[1] *The Life of William Morris*, by J. W. Mackail, London, 1899, vol. i, p. 8.

lar illustrations than in general discussion, it may be worth while to follow up the survey of the situation which has just been given with an account in detail of the history of a special class of words. In this once prevailed the tendency to bring about absolute uniformity. The movement was arrested before the desired result was attained. It left a few over thirty examples as exceptions to the general practice. In the derivatives of some of these it went back to the regular rule and consequently contributed exceptions to the exceptions. This condition of things has endeared these anomalies to the hearts of thousands. The class itself consists of the words ending in *or* or *our*. About the proper way of spelling this termination controversy has raged for more than a hundred years. The examination of the whole class can be best carried on by selecting one of the words belonging to it as typical of all. To its story the next chapter will be largely confined.

CHAPTER IV

THE QUESTION OF *HONOR*

"WELL, honor is the subject of my story," says Cassius to Brutus, in his effort to persuade his friend to join the conspiracy against the dictator. It was h-o-n-o-r however that he spoke of, not h-o-n-o-u-r. So the word appeared in the folio of 1623, in which the play of *Julius Cæsar* was published for the first time. Unfortunately, the spelling of Shakespeare has not escaped the tampering to which that of nearly all our authors has been subjected by unscrupulous modern editors and publishers. Take the following speech of Brutus, found shortly before the line already quoted, as it is printed in the original edition:

Set Honor in one eye and Death i' th' other,
And I will looke on both indifferently;
For let the Gods so speed mee, as I loue
The name of Honor, more then I feare death.

In defiance of the authority of Shakespeare, so far as it is represented by the folio of 1623,

194

honor in the passages cited above appears in modern editions as *honour*. This spelling did not make its appearance in them until comparatively late. In the second folio of 1632 the word was still *honor*. So it remained in the third folio of 1663–64. It was not till the edition of 1685, the last and poorest of the folios, that the corrupt form *honour* displaced in these passages the original form *honor*. There it has since been generally, if not universally, retained.

It is fair to say that in this method of spelling the word the usage of Shakespeare was far from invariable. Either one of the two forms just given seems to have been used by him indifferently, just as they were by his contemporaries. In his writings *honor*, either as a verb or noun, occurs very nearly seven hundred times. According to the sufficient authority of the New Historical English Dictionary, the spelling *honor* in the folio of 1623 was "about twice as frequent as *honour*." This confirms my own impressions; but these were based merely upon the examination of only about a hundred passages of the seven hundred in which the word occurs. Furthermore, Shakespeare's practice varied widely in the use of individual words of this class, as exemplified in the two poems he himself published. *Humor* appears in them

twice.   In both instances it is without the *u*—
once in *Venus and Adonis*,[1] once in *The Rape
of Lucrece*.[2]   Such also is the spelling of the
word the two times it is found in the *Sonnets*,[3]
but there this fact does not make certain the
practice of the poet.   On the other hand, *labor*,
either as a noun or verb, appears seven times
in the two pieces just mentioned.   Six times out
of the seven it is spelled *labour*.[4]   *Color* also appears invariably as *colour* in the ten times the
word is found in these same poems.

The words with the terminations *or* or *our*
number now several hundred in our speech.
Many of them go back to that early period when
the French element was first introduced into
English.   Many others have been added at various periods since.   In the case of those of
earlier introduction both terminations are found.
Still, it is the impression produced upon me by
my comparatively little reading that there was
at first a distinct preference for the ending *our*.
This, if true, was due largely, if not mainly, to
the fact that it reflected more accurately the then
prevailing pronunciation.   The accent fell upon

---

[1] Line 850.   [2] Line 1825.
[3] *Sonnets* 91 and 92.
[4] *Venus and Adonis*, lines 969, 976; *The Rape of
Lucrece*, 1099, 1290, 1380, 1506; in line 586 it is *labor*.

the end of the word.   It was not, as now, thrown
back upon the penult or antepenult, with the
result of placing only the slightest of stress upon
the final syllable.   However this may be, many
words were once often spelled with the termina
tion *our*, which have now replaced it by the
termination *or*.   The ryme-index to Chaucer's
poetry shows that he uses about forty words
with this ending at the close of a line.   Some
are obsolete, but most are still in current use.
Among these latter so spelled are *ambassadour*,
confessour, *emperour*, *governour*, *mirrour*, *sena-
tour*, *servitour*, *successour*, and *traitour*.   These
in modern English have replaced the ending
our by *or*.   Again other words with this same
terminations which he employs have now substituted for it *er*.   Such are *reportour*, *revelour*,
and *riotour*.   In truth, each one of the words
belonging to the class has a history of its own.
But *honor* is in most respects typical of them all.
Accordingly, while there is no purpose to neglect
the others, upon it the attention will be mainly
fixed.

   It was in the fourteenth century that the
wholesale irruption of the French element into
our vocabulary took place.   But before the great
invasion in which words came into the speech
by battalions, single words had already entered,

as if to prepare the way. One of these earlier adventurers was the term under consideration. It made its appearance in the language as early, at least, as the beginning of the thirteenth century. Unlike most of its class, its first syllable demands attention as well as its last. As a foreign word, it naturally exhibited at its original introduction the forms that belonged to it in the tongue from which it was derived. There was no prejudice in those days in favor of a fixed orthography. Each author did what was right in his own eyes; or perhaps it would be more correct to say, what was right to his own ears. In the Romance tongues the hostility to the aspirate, which has animated the hearts of so large a share of the race, had caused it to be dropped in pronunciation. As a result, writers being then phonetically inclined, discarded it from the spelling. Hence, *honor* presented itself in our language without the initial *h*. Its first recorded appearance is in a work, the manuscript of which is ascribed to the neighborhood of 1200 A.D. In that it was written *onur*, just as *hour* sometimes appeared as *ure*. It hardly needs to be said that the vowel in these cases does not represent the now common sound we call "short *u*."

It is not always easy to discover the motives

which influence men in the choice of spellings. But it is no difficult matter to detect the reason for the change which here took place. Before the minds of the writers of this early period was always the Latin original. In that tongue the word began with *h*. Derivation is always dear to the hearts of the scholastically inclined. In those days it was only men of this class who did any writing at all. Hence, both in Old French and in Old English, it was not long before the letter *h* came to be prefixed regularly to the word. It was not sounded. But it was soon adopted universally in the spelling, and, once established there, it never lost its hold. In the case of several other words which have had essentially the same history, the pronunciation of the aspirate has been resumed under the influence of the printed page. But *honor* is one of four which up to this time have held out unflinchingly against any such tendency.

So much for the initial letter. As regards the termination, the word made its appearance in several forms. Only three of them need be mentioned here, for they were the ones much the most common. These were *honor*, *honour*, *honur*. The last was the first to go. It left the field to the other two forms, which have flourished side by side from that day to this.

Were I to trust to the impressions produced by my own reading, I should say that from the middle of the fourteenth century to the middle of the sixteenth the form in *our* was much the more common. But, in the New Historical English Dictionary, Dr. Murray asserts distinctly that "*honor* and *honour* continued to be equally frequent down to the seventeenth century." One accordingly must defer to the authority of a generalization which is based upon a much fuller array of facts than it is in the power of an individual to get together.

By the time we reach the sixteenth century, and especially the Elizabethan age, it is pretty plain that something of the orthographic controversy which has been raging ever since had already begun to make itself heard. The little we know about it we learn from brief remarks in books or chance allusions in plays. The discussion, such as it was, seems to have had little regard to orthoepy, but was based almost entirely upon considerations of etymology. It was in the sixteenth century more particularly that derivation began to work havoc with the spelling. Sometimes it simplified it; full as frequently, if not more frequently, it perverted what little phonetic character words had possessed originally or had been enabled to retain.

For the classical influence was then at its height. Consequently, a disposition was apt to manifest itself to go back to the Latin form and insert letters which had been dropped from the spelling because they had been dropped from the pronunciation.

It seems inevitable that the etymological bias so prevalent in the sixteenth century should have exerted some influence, and perhaps a good deal of influence, in causing a preference to be given by many to the forms in *or*. Old French had been forgotten by the community generally, and met the eyes of lawyers only. Modern French had not then so much vogue as Italian. But Latin was familiar to every educated man. It was accordingly natural that the spelling of the words of the class under consideration should show a tendency to go back to the forms employed in that tongue. This inference may seem to be borne out by the few specific data which have been collected. In the case of Shakespeare the existence of a concordance to his writings enables us to furnish certain positive statements with comparative ease. Mention has been made of the fact that in the folio of 1623 the spelling *honor* occurs twice as often as *honour*. Of course, in a work printed so long after his death, this is no positive evidence as to the dramatist's own usage. But whatever preference he felt, it seems right to infer, was indicated in the two poems published in his lifetime. Of these the proofs must have passed under his own eye. In *The Rape of Lucrece*, which came out in 1594, the word occurs just twenty times: in seventeen instances it is spelled *honor;* in three, *honour.* In *Venus and Adonis* it is found but twice. In both instances *honor* is the spelling employed.

A generalization, however, based upon isolated facts is always liable to be misleading. Whatever value attaches to those just given is due mainly to the eminence of the author. No statement of universal, or even of common usage can be safely based upon them.[1] The examination of other books would in all likelihood show divergence in many instances from the practice here indicated. Furthermore, we must not forget that English orthography is not due to scholars or men of letters, but to typesetters. The spellings found in any book of the Elizabethan period are as likely to be

[1] In the original edition of *The Rape of Lucrece, honor* is found in lines 45, 142, 146, 156, 574, 579, 834, 841, 842, 1031, 1032, 1184, 1186, 1190, 1201, 1608, and 1705; *honour* is found in lines 27, 145, and 516. In *Venus and Adonis* the word occurs in lines 558 and 994, both times as *honor.*

those of the printing-house as of the author. This, in fact, is not unfrequently true of our own age. It is likewise clear that these same printing-houses exhibited a fine impartiality in the use of these terminations. Volume after volume can be taken up, on different pages of which we can find *honor* and *honour*, *humor*, and *humour*, *labor* and *labour*, and so on through the list. In truth, the book would be an exception where absolute uniformity prevailed.

An interesting example of this variableness of usage may be observed in the dozen lines in which Shakespeare dedicated, in 1593, his poem of *Venus and Adonis* to the Earl of Southampton. The inscription is to the "Right Honorable Henrie Wriothesley"; the address itself begins with "Right Honourable." Throughout these few lines the phrase "your honor" occurs just three times. Twice it is spelled *honor*, once *honour*. Modern editions entirely ignore this variation of usage. In every instance they insert the *u* in the word, thus giving, as usual, to the modern reader an entirely false impression of Shakespeare's practice.

In this matter the only incontrovertible fact to be found is that in the late sixteenth and early seventeenth centuries both *honor* and *honour* exist side by side. Which form occurs more frequently in the period could not be told without an exhaustive investigation of its whole literature. As a result of my own necessarily incomplete observation, I should say that from the middle of the seventeenth century there was a growing sentiment in favor of the ending *our* in the majority of dissyllabic words. This tendency became distinctly stronger after the Restoration. On the other hand, the disposition to use the form in *or* became increasingly prevalent in words of more than two syllables. To both these statements there are exceptions, perhaps numerous exceptions, especially in the case of the latter. Individual, preferences, too counted for a great deal in an age when the idolatrous devotion to our present orthography had not begun to manifest itself. But the statements just given may be taken as a near approach to the truth, if not the precise truth itself.

Assuredly the tendency to use the forms in *our* increased in the latter half of the seventeenth century. This was: true in particular of dissyllabic words. In the years which followed the Restoration it seems to have become dominant. Such a conclusion is apparently supported by the dictionaries of the time. Let us go back for evidence to our title-word. The spelling *honour* is the only one authorized in the dictionaries of Phillips, Kersey, Coles, Fenning, and Martin, which appeared during the latter part of the seventeenth century or the earlier part of the eighteenth. It has already been mentioned that before the publication of Doctor Johnson's, the two leading authorities were Bailey's and Dyche and Pardon's. Of the two, the latter was probably the less widely used. Bailey gave to these now disputed words the ending in *our*. He did not even recognize the existence of that in *or*. On the other hand, Dyche, in the case of certain of them, authorized both forms. He put down, for example, *honor* and *honour*, *error* and *errour*, *humor* and *humour*. Furthermore, in each of these instances he gave the preference to the first. Of course, he was not thoroughgoing in his practice. He would have been unfaithful to the national spirit had he been consistent. Accordingly, in other words of this class, such as *favor* and *labor*, he recognized only the spelling in *our*.

But as in every period there are found those who cherish with peculiar affection whatever is anomalous or incongruous or irrational, and cling to it through good report and evil report, so there always spring up a pestilent crowd of men who have an abiding hostility to whatever displays these characteristics. The attention of certain restless beings of this sort began to be directed toward this very class of words. By the middle of the eighteenth century their influence was making itself felt. A perceptible disposition was manifested to do away with the irregularities that had come to prevail. It does not seem to have been based upon any phonetic grounds. It apparently owed little or nothing to the desire to conform to the Latin original. The aim seems simply to have been to simplify orthography by reducing all the words of this class to a uniform termination. At this time polysyllables belonging to it— the trisyllables being included under that term —had largely come to drop the *u*. So had a respectable number of dissyllables. Why not make the rule universal? Why add to the difficulty inherent in English orthography the further difficulty of an arbitrary distinction which serves no useful purpose? No particular reason seemed to exist why *author* and *error* should be spelled without *u*, and *honor* and *favor* and *color* with it. So they argued. The movement for dropping the vowel made distinct headway; it actually accomplished a good deal, and might have accomplished everything had it not met the powerful opposition of Doctor Johnson. In 1755 came out his dictionary. It did not drive out of circulation other works of the same kind, but it largely deprived them of authority with the educated. It practically gained the position of a court of final appeal.

Johnson knew very little about orthoepy and its relation to orthography; but on account of the deference paid to him, not only by his contemporaries, who knew nothing whatever about either, but also by later lexicographers, especially the two most prominent, Sheridan and Walker, his work is of very great importance for the influence it has had upon English spelling. Toward most of what he recommended a sort of religious respect was soon exhibited by many. This attitude may be said to have characterized for a long time the English people. He set himself against the processes of simplification that were going on. He laid down the dictum that the true orthography must always be regarded as dependent upon the derivation. It must, therefore, be determined by its immediate original. He did not conform to his own theory; he could not conform to it. But men accepted his assertions without paying any special heed to his practice. In consequence, his authority exerted a distinct influence toward retaining many spellings which in his time were tending to go out of use.

Especially was this true of the words of the class under consideration. At the time Johnson was engaged in the preparation of his dictionary the forms in *or* had come to be in a distinct majority. Usage was variable, it is true, depending as it did on individual likes or dislikes. But on the whole a preference was beginning to manifest itself for the termination *or*, at least outside of certain words. Still, it would have been then possible to bring about uniformity by the adoption of either ending to the exclusion of the other. From the orthographical point of view of that period, no serious objection would have been offered by the large majority of men to that course of action. But such a proceeding would, in the eyes of many, have been attended with one fatal defect. It would have made the termination of all the words of this class uniform, and therefore easy to understand and to master. This would have brought the result into conflict with the cherished though unavowed ideal we hold, which is to make the spelling as difficult of acquisition as possible. In this feeling Johnson himself unconsciously shared. He had to the full that love of the illogical and anomalous and unreasonable, with the contributing fondness for half-measures, which is so characteristic of our race as contrasted with the French. This attitude was reflected in his treatment of this particular class of words. He compromised the controversy between the two endings in the case of about a hundred of the most common of them by impartially spelling about half with *or* and the other half with *our*.

Furthermore, in regard to the particular class of words under discussion, both Johnson's theory and practice must be taken into consideration. Between these there was wide divergence, and oftentimes contradiction. In theory he set himself resolutely against the efforts of those who were seeking to bring about uniformity. He pointed out that "*our* is frequently used in the last syllable of words which in Latin end in *or*, and are made English as *honour, labour, favour*, for *honor, labor, favor*." He then set out to give the reasons for his own choice of the form he had adopted. "Some late innovators," he wrote, "have ejected the *u*, not considering that the last syllable gives the sound neither of *o* nor *u*, but a sound between them, if not compounded of both." The just observation contained in one part of this sentence is rendered nugatory by the unfounded assertion at the end and the extraordinary conclusion drawn. Johnson's argument really amounts to this: Neither *o* nor *u* represents the actual vowel sound heard in the last syllable. In each case there would be only an approach to it. Therefore, let us not think of employing either one of the vowels which represent the sound only imperfectly, but a vowel combination which does not represent it at all.

His cautiously guarded utterance shows that Johnson was vaguely conscious of the weakness of the position he had taken if not of its absurdity. Hence, he felt the need of furnishing it additional support. So he abandoned phonetics and resorted to derivation. He proceeded to suggest a reason which since his day has played the most important of parts in all the attempts which have been made to explain the cause of the retention of *our* in the spelling of these words. "Besides that," he continued, "they are probably derived from the French nouns in *eur*, as *honeur* (*sic*), *faveur*." Johnson had not that courage of his ignorance which distinguishes the assertions of later men who employ his argument. He spoke hesitatingly of the derivation as a probability. As it was erroneous, this course was wise. His followers, however, from that day to this, have invariably stated it as a fact. He repeated, nevertheless, his general view in the grammar with which he prefaced the dictionary. "Some ingenious men," he remarked, sarcastically, "have endeavored to deserve well of their country by writing *honor* and *labor* for *honour* and *labour.*"

Such was Johnson's attitude in theory; his action was distinctly different. Like the rest of us, he was governed entirely by sentiment working independently of knowledge or reason. He preferred the spelling, as do we all, which he himself was wont to use. He judged it to be the proper spelling because he was familiar with it. The utter lack of any intelligent or even intelligible principle he was actuated by in his choice can be illustrated by two or three examples. *Anterior* was spelled by him with the ending *our; posterior* with the ending *or.* The termination of *interior* was *our;* that of *exterior* was *or.* This is not the reign of law, but of lawlessness. The only explanation I have been able to devise of the motives, outside of association, which may have unconsciously led him to adopt the ending he did in any particular case, was a possible feeling on his part that when the word denoted the agent it should have the termination *or;* but *our* when it denoted state or condition. This is not a satisfactory reason for making a difference; but it has a glimmering of sense. Yet while in general this course is true of Johnson's practice, it is, unfortunately, not universally true. *Stupor* and *torpor* appeared, for illustration, in his dictionary without the *u;* while on the other hand with it are found *ambassadour, emperour, governour,* and *warriour.*

It is certain that Johnson himself, in the spellings he authorized, never conformed to the principle of derivation, which he held out to us as the all-sufficient guide. Several of the words which appear in his dictionary with the intruding vowel had come to us directly from the Latin. Accordingly, the form he gave them was in direct defiance of the principles which he had laid down. Of these *candor* is so striking an example that it is worth while to give some account of it in detail. The word came into our language in the fourteenth century, but as a pure Latin word. When used in the black-letter period, after the invention of printing, it appeared in Roman type, to indicate that it was still a foreigner, just as we now indicate a borrowed term by italics. In the early seventeenth century it had become naturalized. Accordingly, it was at first spelled like its original. About the middle of the seventeenth century *u* was occasionally inserted. This way of spelling it increased after the Restoration. Necessarily, such a usage not only defied but disguised the real original. For a long time the correct and incorrect forms flourished side by side. It was Johnson's adoption of the ending *our* for the word which fixed this erroneous spelling upon the English people. Men now tell you with all the intense earnestness of ignorance that *candor* should be spelled with a *u* because it came from a foreign word which has no direct connection with it whatever. Yet the very same men who insist upon retaining a *u* in *honor*, because, as they fancy, it was derived from the French *honneur*, cling just as tenaciously to the form *candour*, and will cling to it after they have learned to know that it was derived directly from the Latin *candor*.

Not only, indeed, in his preaching, but in his personal practice, Johnson may be said to have been inconsistent in his inconsistency. Of this there is a most singular illustration. In the dictionary itself *author* was given as here spelled. Not even a hint was conveyed of the existence of another form. But in the preface to the dictionary this same word was employed by him just fourteen times. In every instance it was spelled *authour*. Nor could this have been the

213

fault of the type-setter. So far was it from exciting remonstrance or reprehension on his part that the form is not only found in the first edition of 1755, but also in the fourth edition of 1773, the last which appeared in his lifetime, and which underwent some slight revision at his hands. Had Johnson chanced to adopt in the body of the work the spelling of this word as it appeared in his preface to it, the form with *u* would in all probability have continued to maintain itself. Men would be found at this day to insist that the very safety of the language depended upon its permanent retention. There would, indeed, be authors who would fail to recognize themselves as authors unless this unnecessary *u* was inserted into the word denoting their profession.

But though the weight of Johnson's authority was impaired by his practice, there is no question that his words did more to prevent the universal adoption of the ending *or* than any other single agency. For that purpose they were timely. There had then begun to be something of an effort to correct certain of the most striking errors and inconsistencies of English orthography. With this, Hume, for one, sympathized. That this assumed enemy of the faith should be favorably inclined to any movement of the sort, and to some extent should conform to it, was enough of itself to set Doctor Johnson against it. That author, in the first edition of his History, had followed what was then sometimes called the new method of spelling. As regards the particular class of words here under consideration, he used several such forms as *ardor, flavor, labor, vigor,* and *splendor.* But Hume had no vital interest in the matter. His reason told him what was proper and analogical; but he was little disposed to fight convention on this point. Therefore, he wavered at intervals between spellings which he recognized as sensible and those which had the approval of the printing-house and consequently that of the general public. "I had once an intention of changing the orthography in some particulars," he wrote, in 1758, to Strahan, on the occasion of bringing out a new edition of his History, " but on reflection I find that this new method of spelling (which is certainly the best and most conformable to analogy) has been followed in the quarto volume of my philosophical writings lately published; and, therefore, I think it will be better for you to continue the spelling as it is." [1]

[1] *Letters of David Hume to William Strahan,* Oxford, 1888, p. 27.

In truth, the moment that Doctor Johnson had set the example of attacking the pestilent disturbers of orthographic peace, a host of imitators were sure to follow in his footsteps. One of these was the physician John Armstrong, who dabbled also, to some extent, in literature. Among other things, he produced one of those ponderous poems in which the eighteenth century abounded, and with which the extremely conscientious student of English literature feels himself under obligation to struggle. He also tried his hand at a volume of short *Sketches and Essays*, as they were called, which came out anonymously. Among them was one on the *Modern Art of Spelling*. In it he attacked with vigor the so-called reformers who were employing the forms *honor*, *favor*, *labor*. Indeed, he apprised us—what otherwise we should hardly have known—that there were then misguided beings who threw out one of the vowels in the termination of words not belonging strictly to the class we are discussing, and wrote *neighbor*, *behavior*, and *endeavur*. Armstrong's little work appeared in 1757; it might have been written yesterday. It displays the same misunderstanding and misconception of the whole subject which characterizes the men of our day, who have the advantage of being heirs to the accumulated ignorance of the past. In places, too, he was as amusing as they. Nothing, he told us, did so much to distinguish his own "as an *unmanly* age"—the italics are his—"as this very aversion to the honest vowel *u*."

Hume's attitude of indifference is manifested in his comments on this volume. He evidently considered himself as one of the men aimed at in its animadversions upon the reformers. In June, 1758, he spoke about the work in a letter to his publisher, Andrew Millar. "I have read," he wrote, "a small pamphlet called *Sketches*, which, from the style, I take to be Doctor Armstrong's, though the public voice gives it to Allan Ramsay. I find the ingenious author, whoever he be, ridicules the new method of spelling, as he calls it; but that method of spelling *honor*, instead of *honour*, was Lord Bolingbroke's, Doctor Middleton's, and Mr. Pope's, besides many other eminent writers. However, to tell truth, I hate to be in any way particular in a trifle; and, therefore, if Mr. Strahan has not printed off above ten or twelve sheets, I should not be displeased if you told him to follow the usual—that is, his own—way of spelling throughout; we shall make the other volumes conformable to it: if he be advanced

farther, there is no great matter."[1]   This is by
no means a solitary instance of the way in which
authors have submitted their own convictions
to the practices of printing-houses and thereby
caused this creation of type-setters we call
English orthography, to be an object of reverent
worship to thousands, who contribute large
sums to convert those bowing down to gods of
wood and stone.

Great, however, as was Johnson's authority,
there was not paid to it at the time unquestion-
ing assent.   The glaring inconsistency between
his principles and his practice made many indis-
posed to accept him as an infallible guide.   Dissent came from two quarters.   There were those
who accepted fully his views as to the propriety
of following the form of the assumed immediate
original.   These not unreasonably looked with
disfavor upon his dereliction in the case of many
words.   Among the recalcitrants was his devoted disciple Boswell.   In 1768 this author
brought out the journal of his tour in Corsica.
In the preface to it he expressed the feelings of
many in his comments upon his master's course
in this matter.   "It may be necessary," he

---

[1] Burton's *Life and Correspondence of David Hume*,
Edinburgh, 1846, vol. ii, p. 43.   Burton changed Hume's
spellings to conform to modern orthography.

wrote, "to say something in defense of my orthography. Of late it has become the fashion to render our language more neat and trim by leaving out *k* after *c*, and *u* in the last syllable of words which used to end in *our*. The illustrious Mr. Samuel Johnson, who has alone executed in England what was the task of whole academies in other countries, has been careful in his dictionary to preserve the *k* as a mark of the Saxon original. He has for the most part, too, been careful to preserve the *u*, but he has also omitted it in several words. I have retained the *k*, and have taken upon me to follow a general rule with regard to words ending in *our*. Wherever a word originally Latin has been transmitted to us through the medium of the French, I have written it with the characteristic *u*. An attention to this may appear trivial. But I own I am one of those who are curious in the formation of language in its various modes, and therefore wish that the affinity of English with other tongues may not be forgotten."

Boswell resembled most of the ardent partisans of the ending *our* in the fact that his curiosity in the formation of language had never been rewarded by any intelligent knowledge of it. The *k* was, in his eyes, a mark of the Saxon original. The only comment that it is necessary to make upon this assertion is that the letter *k* was not in the Anglo-Saxon alphabet any more than it was in the Roman, from which the former was derived. Hence, as has been already pointed out, monosyllabic words like *back*, *sack*, *sick*, *thick*, in the earliest form of our speech, ended with *c;* and if we were really so devoted to derivation as we pretend, we should have to discard the *k* from the end of monosyllables, just as we have from the end of polysyllables. Boswell, however, carried out his views to their logical conclusion. Johnson might exhibit the weakness of deferring in particular instances to general custom; not so his follower and admirer. So we find him running counter to his master's teachings by using the spellings *authour*, *doctour*, *rectour*, *taylour*, and others among the dissyllables; and among the polysyllables there were the forms *professour*, *spectatour*, *conspiratour*, *preceptour*, *innovatour*, *legislatour*, and a large number that need not be given here.

It is evident from Boswell's protest that the disposition to drop the *u* had become so prevalent that there was danger of its prevailing. The aversion was increasing to the use of this very honest letter, as Armstrong had called it. Johnson's authority retarded the progress of this tendency, but outside of a certain limited number of cases did not check it effectually. It was not long before the vowel was pretty regularly dropped in polysyllabic words. In them it has remained dropped ever since. Few, indeed, are the persons who can now be found writing *ambassadour, emperour, governour, oratour, possessour*, and no small number of others which the great lexicographer insisted upon as the proper way. Even some of his dissyllabic words have gone over to the form in *or*, notably those which had *rr* before the suffix, such as *error, horror*, and *terror*.

No idea of the strength of the movement towards uniformity can be gathered from the dictionaries of the time. These, as a general rule, followed Johnson even when the rest of the world was going the other way. Both Sheridan and Walker stuck to the final *k* long after nearly everybody else had given it up. The latter, indeed, deplored the custom of omitting it because it had introduced into the language the novelty of ending a word with an unusual letter. This, on the face of it, he said, was a blemish. Still less did the lexicographers represent the general attitude of the time towards the class of words here considered, especially the attitude of aristocratic society. The fortunes of two of these words, in particular, on account of the frequency of their appearance on cards of invitation, reached at this period the highest social elevation. These were *honor* and *favor*. To spell them with a *u* became and remained for a long while a distinctive mark of rusticity and illbreeding—not, as now, an evidence of imperfect acquaintance with their history.

On this point we have plenty of unimpeachable testimony. The dictionary of Walker, the leading lexicographer of his own generation and of the generation following, came out towards the end of the eighteenth century. In it he gave utterance to his grief on this very subject. His remarks occur under the word of which, in defiance of general custom, he continued to authorize the form *honour*. "This word," he said, "and its companion *favour*, the two servile attendants upon cards and notes of fashion, have so generally dropped the *u* that to spell these words with that letter is looked upon as *gauche* and rustick in the extreme. In vain did Dr. Johnson enter his protest against the innovation; in vain did he tell us that the sound of the word required the use of *u*, as well as its derivation from the Latin through the French: the sentence seems to have been passed, and we now hardly even find these words with this vowel but in dictionaries."

SPELLING REFORM

But Walker, though he followed, as in duty
bound, his great leader, was subject to qualms of
common sense.   These, when they occur, always
make sad work with orthographic prejudices.
When he looked at the matter dispassionately he
had to confess that Johnson's arguments in behalf of the spellings which he had authorized did
not impress him altogether favorably; in fact,
he manifested a sneaking inclination for the
forms without *u*.   "Though," he said, "I am
a declared enemy to all needless innovation, I
see no inconvenience in spelling these words in
the fashionable manner: there is no reason for
preserving the *u* in *honour* and *favour* that does
not hold good for the preservation of the same
letter in *errour*, *authour*, and a hundred others;
and with respect to the pronunciation of these
words without *u*, while we have so many words
where the *o* sounds *u*, even when the accent is
on it, as *honey*, *money*, etc., we need not be in
much pain for the sound of *u*, in words of this
termination, where the final *r* brings all the accented vowels to the same level; that is, the
short sound of *u*."

The fashionable method of spelling these
words prevailed for a long time.   The behavior
of high society in so doing stirred profoundly
the deep-seated conservatism of the middle

223

class. The great founder of Methodism warned his followers against this vanity. "Avoid," wrote Wesley, in 1791, "the fashionable impropriety of leaving out the *u* in many words, as *honor, vigor*, etc. This is mere childish affectation." Remarks of this sort availed nothing—at least, they did not affect the right persons. The aristocratic world cared little for the woes of lexicographers or the denunciations of religious leaders. As is its wont, it went on in its usual heartless way, paying no heed whatever to the remonstrances directed against its conduct in this matter.

The practice seems to have continued during the first third, at least, of the nineteenth century. As late as 1832 Archdeacon Hare denounced it in the Philological Museum. Hare was, in his way, a spelling-reformer, and drew upon himself much obloquy for the orthographical peculiarities he adopted. He furnished us himself with some specimens of the sort of objections which were raised to his efforts. As might be expected, they were made up of the same old combination of virulence and ignorance with which we are all familiar. In the eyes of one, change of spelling was a piece of impudent presumption. In the eyes of another, it was a piece of silly affectation. Or, again, it was a mistaking of singularity for originality, a waste upon trifles of attention which ought to be reserved for matters of real importance. What surprises us now is that so much excitement should have been provoked by alterations so petty; for all of any importance that Hare proposed was spelling the participial ending *ed* as *t* when it had the sound of *t*. Thus, we find in his writings *reacht, vanquisht, pickt, supprest, rusht, publisht*, and no small number of similar forms. These he defended, as it was easy to do, by the usage of Spenser and Milton and their contemporaries—even, indeed, from the practice of the comic dramatists who followed the Restoration period, such as Congreve, Vanbrugh, and Farquhar. That petty changes of this nature should have been regarded by educated men as serious innovations shows how all-extensive had become with them the ignorance of the history of their own tongue.

Hare's countrymen ought, indeed, to have been reassured by his other spellings that there was no danger of immediate ruin to the language by any innovations he might be supposed to favor. The truth is that he knew almost as little of the real principles governing orthography and talked of them nearly as much as did his friend and fellow-reformer, Walter Savage

Landor. But however perverse were his vagaries in other matters, upon the class of words ending in *or* or *our* he was, unlike Landor, eminently sound. Indeed, he was more than sound. He reintroduced the *u* into some words of this class where it had at one time often appeared but had then become generally discarded. He trotted out, as was in those days almost inevitable, the old bugaboo of derivation, as unconscious of its erroneousness, scholar as he was, as are now the most unscholarly who persist in obtruding it upon a generation which knows better. "If," he wrote, "*honour*, *favour*, and other similar words had come to us directly from the Latin, it might be better to spell them without a *u;* but since we got them through the French, so that they brought the *u* with them when they landed on our shores, it will be well to leave such affectations as *honor* and *favor* to the great vulgar for their cards of invitation."

The concluding sentence of this quotation shows conclusively that with people of high position—"the great vulgar," as Hare calls them—fashion at the close of the first third of the last century still dictated the use of the spellings *honor* and *favor*. Herein Hare was opposed to his fellow-reformer Landor. "We

226

differ," says the latter, "on the spelling of *honour*, *favour*, etc. You would retain the *u*; I would eject it for the sake of consistency."[1] If Landor can be trusted to have given a faithful picture of contemporary practice, this method of spelling must have continued for at least a score of years after the date already given. In 1846 came out the third edition of his *Imaginary Conversations*. To the dialogue on language which is represented as having taken place between Doctor Johnson and John Horne Tooke, he added then a number of passages. Among them was the following:

Tooke. Would there be any impropriety or inconvenience in writing *endevor* and *demeanor*, as we write *tenor*, without the *u?*
Johnson. Then you would imitate cards of invitation, where we find *favor* and *honor*.
Tooke. We find *ancestor* and *author* and *editor* and *inventor* in the works of Dr. Johnson, who certainly bears no resemblance to a card of invitation. Why can we not place all these words on the same bench?

But fashion comes and goes, while the dictionaries are ever present. As a rule, lexicographers are a timid race of men. They have little

[1] *Imaginary Conversations.* Archdeacon Hare and Walter Landor.

227

disposition to deviate from the paths marked out by their predecessors. Even the revision of Dyche's work, which appeared toward the end of the eighteenth century, discarded his alternative use of *honor*, to which it had once given the first place, though at the time itself this usage had become fashionable. So far as I have observed, the only eighteenth-century lexicographer after Johnson who fell in with the current tendency was Ash, whose dictionary first appeared in 1775. He entered separately the two forms of these words, giving, for illustration, *honor*, *color*; and *labor* as "the modern and correct spelling," and *honour*, *colour*, and *labour* as "the old and usual spelling." But his action availed little against the agreement of the others; for apparently, with this exception, the dictionaries stood their ground manfully. Their combined authority had necessarily a good deal of effect upon the general practice, especially with that numerous class of men who did not feel themselves familiar enough with the subject to act independently.

At a still later period international prejudice came in to strengthen the disposition in England to stand by the letter *u* in the comparatively few cases in which it had continued to survive. In America, Webster had thrown out

the vowel in all words of this class. In so doing
he was followed, half apologetically, by Worcester. Their agreement had the effect of making
the practice of dispensing with the *u* almost universal in this country. One singular result of
it was that in time the termination in *or* instead
of *our* came to be considered an American innovation. To this very day the delusion prevails widely on both sides of the Atlantic that
the form of a word which entered the language
more than two centuries before America was
discovered, which has been in more or less use
in every century since its introduction, owed
its existence to an American lexicographer.
Naturally this was enough to condemn it in the
eyes of any self-respecting Englishman. The
belief just mentioned has been a very real
though unacknowledged reason for retaining
in that country the termination in *our*. Have
we not been told again and again in countless
English periodicals — quarterlies, monthlies,
weeklies—that Britons will never, never tolerate
any such hideous monstrosity as the American
spelling, *honor* ?

But whatever may have been the causes which
brought about, or concurred to bring about, the
reaction in this matter which took place in
Great Britain, there is no question whatever as

to the fact. The tendency, once prevalent and steadily increasing, to drop the *u* from all the words of this class, as they had been dropped from most, was effectually arrested. Even the lexicographers who could see no sense in the maintenance of this inconsistency in the spelling accepted it while they deplored it. After the passing of Walker, Smart's remodelling of his dictionary became, in the middle of the nineteenth century, the leading orthographic authority in use in England. The reviser recognized the absurdity of the disagreement which prevailed in the spelling of this class of words. Still, he saw no way of remedying it. In describing his method of dealing with them, he remarked that he might have followed Webster's course, and adopted throughout the termination *or*. This clearly struck him as sensible, but he as clearly felt that it would never do. "Such, however," he wrote, "is not the practice of the day, though some years ago there was a great tendency towards it." For in the meantime a peculiar regard for these exceptions to the general rule had sprung up among the orthographically uneducated, a class to which most educated men belong. These exceptions were not very numerous. They were all dissyllabic words; for the retention of the *u* in the polysyllables was too much for even the Anglo-Saxon love of the anomalous. Still, for the comparatively few exceptions which had been saved from the general wreck which had overtaken the *our* forms, there had begun to display itself that peculiar enthusiastic zeal which always prevails when devotion defies reason. No one assuredly can maintain that the latter quality exists in an orthography which insists upon inserting a *u* into *honor* and withholding it from *horror*.

A few more than thirty words in common use have partially outlived the revolution that has brought the vast majority to the termination in *or*. They constitute, in consequence, a limited body of exceptions to the general rule. As in every case the spelling of the particular word must be learned by itself, they together contribute an additional perplexity to the existing perplexities of English orthography. In certain cases they are enabled to interpose a further obstacle in the path of the learner. When he comes to the derivatives of several of them which are spelled in *our* he is called upon to master exceptions to the exceptions. In order to save the language from ruin, he is assured that he must be careful to insert a *u* in *clamor;* but when it comes to *clamorous*, he must be equally careful to leave the *u* out. The same sort of statement can be made of several other words of this same class. We can pardon *laborious* from *labour*. But what excuse can be offered for writing *humour* and then *humorous*, *odour* and then *odorous*, *rancour* and then *rancorous*, *rigour* and then *rigorous*, *valour* and then *valorous*, *vigour* and then *vigorous?* Yet this business of making a still more inextricable muddle out of the already muddled condition of English spelling is held up to us as something essential to the purity and perfection of English speech.

It is assumptions of this sort that are irritating. In an orthography where so much is lawless, there is no need of becoming excited over some particular one of its numerous vagaries. What is offensive in the spelling of *honor* as *honour* is not the termination itself, but the reasons paraded for its adoption. A man can cling to the form with *u* because he has been taught so to spell it, because by constant association he has come to prefer it. To this there may be no objection. But there is distinct objection to his implying, and sometimes asserting, that in so spelling the word he is upholding the purity of the speech. This is to give to his perhaps excusable ignorance the quality of inexcusable impudence. His fancied linguistic virtue is based upon fallacious assumptions which are themselves based upon facts that are false.

Even were the facts true, they would not justify what is inferred from them. The argument for insisting upon the ending *our*, drawn from derivation, might seem to have been fully disposed of in the account of the introduction of this word into English, and of the various forms which it then assumed. But, in spite of the poet, it is error, not truth, which crushed to earth rises again. Men, presumably of intelligence, continue still to repeat the assertion that the word should be spelled *honour* because it came from the French *honneur*. The proclaimers of this view seem honestly to think that the lives of all of us would be irremediably saddened did not the presence of the *u* in this particular English word remind us of its assumed French original; though the absence of the *u* in no small number of words with the same termination, and having essentially the same history, does not seem to cause in any of us etymological depression of spirit. But even in this instance deference to derivation manifestly does not go far enough. If we are to write *honour* because it came from the French *honneur*,

233

what excuse can be offered for omitting the *e*?
Even more, what excuse can be offered for
omitting one of the two *n's*? Assuredly there
is no sacredness belonging to the vowel which
does not attach also to the consonant. The
happiness of the devotee of derivation would
be still further enhanced by spelling the word
honnour; in fact, in the sixteenth century this
was occasionally done.

The real objection, however, to this particular argument for the spelling *honour* is that it
has not a particle of truth in it. It is based
entirely upon complete ignorance of the facts.
Neither *honor* nor *honour* was derived from
honneur. It is doubtful if that French form
existed when *honor* came into the English language. However that may be, such was not
the form in Anglo-French from which the English word descended. In that it was sometimes
spelled *honor*. From it so spelled came our one
modern form. In that again it was sometimes
spelled *honour*. From it so spelled came our
other modern form. The English word had,
therefore, a history independent of the French.
Its development took place not on the same but
on a parallel line. Under these circumstances
there is something peculiarly ridiculous in the
assertion so constantly made, that if the *u*

were dropped from *honor*, the history of the word would be lost.

There still remains to be noticed an objection —the utmost strength of the human imagination cannot well term it an argument — which has been raised against the spelling in *or* in such words as have succeeded to a certain extent in retaining the *u*. It is that a change of this sort is certain in some undefined way to ruin the nobler sentiments of the soul. It is conceded that the *u* contributes nothing to the pronunciation of the word, but it conduces to the edification and spiritual elevation of him who is particular to insert it. It is intimated by such as take this view that it is not those who belong to the cold, proud world who could share in this sentiment or rather sentimentality. Still less would it weigh with those mechanical utilitarians who think it enough to be guided in their spelling by sense and reason. To them no ray of the divine rapture has been imparted which transports the heart of him who finds his whole nature expand at the presence of a *u* in *honor* and *favor* and chilled by its absence. Let no one fancy that this sort of objection is too ridiculous to be advanced seriously. There has not been a discussion of spelling reform in modern times in which it has not been brought forward. In the case of those who have taken part in the latest controversy, I have already expressed my unwillingness to employ that severest form of personal attack which consists in citing their own words. I shall accordingly confine myself here to some remarks of this sort which were made more than a quarter of a century ago. In 1873 a controversy was going on in England as to the proper way of spelling the *or, our* class of words. In the course of it a correspondent sent to the periodical entitled *Notes and Queries* a communication which contained the following exalted sentiments:

"I think that *honour* has a more noble and *favour* a more obliging look than *honor* and *favor*. *Honor* seems to me to do just his duty and nothing more; *favor* to qualify his kind deed with an air of coldness. *Odor*, again, may be a fit term for a chemical distillation; but a whole May garden comes before me in the word *odour*."

The lover of the classics must always feel a sense of regret that Cicero and Virgil and Horace were denied by the spelling prevailing in their tongue the opportunity of enjoying this May garden, so cheaply secured for this sentimental Englishman by spelling *odor* with a *u*. It is al-

ways unfortunate when the sense of largeness of
soul can only be developed at the expense of intellect.   Fanciful notions like the one just cited
can never be dispelled by argument, as reason
plays no part in bringing them into being.   As
to association alone they owe their creation, so
to association alone will they owe their destruction.

CHAPTER V

METHODS OF RELIEF

HE who has taken the pains to master the details given in the chapter on English sounds and the signs which are intended to represent them, will have received some conception of the nature of the orthographic slough in which we are wallowing, and also of the difficulty which exists of getting out of it. He will recognize that the obstacles which stand in the way of the reform of English spelling are not merely greater in number but are harder to overcome than those which beset any other cultivated tongue of modern Europe. Incomplete as is the survey, it is a melancholy picture which it presents. To him who has not become so accustomed to disorder that he has learned to love it for its own sake, the view is distinctly disheartening. The present orthography fulfills neither its legitimate office of denoting pronunciation nor its illegitimate one of disclosing derivation. It is consistent only in inconsistency. It is not necessary for us to consider here how this state of things came about. It is enough to know that it exists. A thoroughgoing reform of English orthography would therefore be one of the most gigantic of enterprises, even if men were fully informed about it and their hearts were set upon it. But a distinct majority of the educated class, though not educated on this subject, are opposed to it. Naturally the profounder their ignorance, the more intense is their hostility. It is no wonder, therefore, that many, in contemplating this dead-weight of prejudice that must be unloaded, have come to despair of the language ever being relieved in the slightest of the burden.

Let it be assumed, however, for the sake of the argument, that a general agreement exists that a reform of some kind is regarded not merely as desirable, but as practicable. At once arises the question: What shall be its nature? How far shall it be carried? Two courses are clearly open. One is to make a thoroughgoing reform of English orthography in order to have it accord with a genuine phonetic ideal, so that when a man sees a word he will know how to pronounce it, and when he hears a word he will know how to spell it. Then harmony between orthography and orthoepy will be complete. Now there is certainly nothing either irrational or of itself offensive in the idea, whatever opinion we may hold as to the practicability or desirability of its attainment. Were we starting out to create a brand-new language, it is not likely that any one would be found wrong-headed or muddle-headed enough to look upon such an aim as improper or unwise. But conceding this ideal to be incapable of realization in the present state of public opinion, there is presented to our consideration the other course. This is to reduce the existing anomalies in our spelling, serving no use and displaying no sense, to the lowest possible number; to discard from words their unneeded and misleading letters; to bring all the words of the same general class under the operation of phonetic law, so as to produce uniformity where an unintelligible diversity now prevails. These are distinct objects. They constitute two separate movements which may be characterized by a slight difference in the wording. One is reform *of* English orthography; the other is reform *in* English orthography.

There have been in the past, and are likely to be in the future, many attempts at solving the perplexing problems involved in the furtherance of the first of these two movements.

Some of them have been logical and consistent throughout. But one difficulty there is which has stood in the way of their acceptance. It will for a long time to come stand in the way. They must necessarily be addressed to generations which have not even an elementary conception of what the sounds of the language are, what are their real values, and what is the proper way of representing these values. As language is now learned full as much by the eye as by the ear, if not, indeed, more so, the form of the word as it is spelled, not as it is pronounced, becomes what is associated in the common mind with the word itself. In modern times this has begot an unreasoning devotion. Accordingly, as difference in a hitherto unheard method of pronunciation has always affected men by the mere sound of it, so does now a new spelling affect them by the sight of it. It arrests the attention of all. Of some it excites the resentment; to others it almost causes convulsions of agony. Hence, those who advocate a pure phonetic spelling—in itself the only strictly rational method—are holding forth a counsel of perfection to a body of persons who are so steeped in orthographic iniquity that they have come to think it the natural condition of the race. This is a situation which has to be recognized.

Therefore, in the present state of public opinion, largely unintelligent and hostile in proportion to its lack of intelligence, it seems to me that reform *of* English orthography—using the distinction just made—is not practicable. We must content ourselves with reform *in* English orthography, imperfect and unsatisfactory in many particulars as it necessarily must be. Still, the middling possible is better than the ideally unattainable.

In a certain sense the latter course is, or ought to be, included in the former. Any reform *in* English orthography which conflicts with the ideal of reform *of* English orthography is not really a reform at all. It is nothing more than a temporary makeshift which puts an obstacle in the way of proper future effort. A piecemeal restoration of anything which is not in full conformity with the just restoration of the whole will do more than leave something to be desired. It will introduce much to be deprecated. Any process of simplification in a language whose spelling is so inherently vicious as ours is sure to be attended with inconsistencies. In any partial reform there will always arise exceptions which can never be swept away until that thorough-going reform is made for which the public mind is not prepared. These exceptions will be seized upon and triumphantly paraded by the opponents of change as proof that as the reform proposed cannot be made perfect at once, it ought not to be begun at all. There would be truth in the last contention if the alterations recommended were not, as far as they go, in full conformity with that phonetic ideal which, though we shall never reach, we ought always to keep in view. The one essential thing to be insisted upon in the reform *in* English orthography is that it shall follow the path of reform *of* English orthography, no matter how far it may lag behind it. There should be no resort to temporary expedients which result in bringing out about a mere external uniformity at the cost of sacrificing the principle that the spelling should represent the sound. Furthermore, it must not bow down to the false god of derivation when such a course brings the form of the word into conflict with its pronunciation.

Much, indeed, of the discredit and ill success which have attended previous efforts in behalf of spelling reform have been due to the imperfect knowledge and erroneous action of those who have undertaken them. They saw that there was an evil; they did not see what the nature of the evil was. Hence, they adopted

243

wrong methods of relief. They did not propose
their half-measures as preparations for something better. They looked upon them as final
in themselves. It need hardly be said that
reform of this particular kind could never
be pressed consciously as reform until after
uniformity of spelling had practically been
established. Consequently, changes *in* orthography, as distinguished from change *of* orthography, can hardly be said to go back to an
early period. Nearly all noteworthy attempts
of the sort took place in the latter half of the
eighteenth century or the former half of the
nineteenth. Johnson's method of spelling was
felt, especially in the earlier of these two periods,
more than it was later, as a tyranny. It was
still so new that all had not become used to it,
and none had learned to love it with the gush-
ing affection of our time. Many there were
who still remembered the former state of free-
dom. A few were found who sought to set up
rival thrones of their own. The crotchets,
moreover, in which individual writers indulged
have been numberless. In the vast majority
of cases the changes proposed by them have
been based upon no scientific principles. Still
less have they been the product of any thoroughly worked-out theory. Accordingly, they have

served little other purpose than to arrest momentarily the attention of the curious, and have had absolutely no influence whatever upon the orthography generally received.

In truth, many of these attempts at reform have been worse than partial. They have been merely in the direction of a mechanical uniformity which was not based in the slightest upon the nature of things. One illustration of this effort to bring about change which was not improvement can be found in the alterations proposed at the end of the eighteenth century by Joseph Ritson. To scholars Ritson is well known as the fiercest of antiquaries, who loved accuracy with the same passion with which other men love persons, and who hated a mistake, whether arising from ignorance or inadvertence, as a saint might hate a deliberate lie. He is equally well known for his devotion to a vegetable diet, and also for the manifestation, noticeable in others so addicted, of a bloodthirstiness of disposition in his criticism which the most savage of carnivorous feeders might have contemplated with envy. The alterations he proposed and carried out in his published works tended in certain ways toward formal regularity; but they also tended to make the divergence between the spelling and the pro-

nunciation still wider. For instance, the so-
called regular verb in our tongue adds *ed* to
form the preterite. Ritson made the general
rule universal. He appended the termination
also to verbs ending in *e*. Accordingly the past
tense, for illustration, of *love, oblige,* and *surprise* appeared as *loveed, obligeed,* and *sur-
priseed*. As nobody pronounces the one *e*
which already exists in these preterites, the insertion of another unnecessary letter could have
only the effect of adding an extra weight to the
burden which these unfortunate words were
carrying as it was.

There were other changes proposed by Ritson.
None were so bad as this, but they were all
valueless. He himself, however, was too
thoroughly honest a man to pretend that he had
arrived at any knowledge of the principles
which underlie the reconstruction of our orthography. He appears at last to have lost all
confid nce in his own alterations. Under his influence his nephew had also been affected with
the fever of reform, and spelled many words in
a way different from that commonly followed.
In a letter written in 1795, Ritson informed his
kinsman that he—the latter—was entirely
ignorant of the principles both of orthography
and of punctuation, and rather wished to be

singular than studied to be right. "For my part," he added, "I am as little fitted for a master as you are for a scholar."

Such changes as those of Ritson provoked amusement rather than opposition. The knowledge of them, indeed, hardly came to the ears of those devoted but never very well-informed idolaters of the existing orthography who feel that the future of the English language and literature depends upon its present spelling, and that the preservation of that spelling in its purity, or, rather, in its impurity, rests largely upon them. They did not attack Ritson's views, because they never heard of them. The changes, again, were too unscientific in their nature to be worthy of serious consideration by him who had the least comprehension of the real difficulties under which our orthography labors. Ritson himself lived long enough not only to doubt the value of his own efforts, but to see that these efforts had been attended by positive pecuniary disadvantage to himself. The worship of the orthographical fetish was then well under way. In a letter to Walter Scott, written in 1803, Ritson told him that his publishers, the Longmans, thought that the orthography made use of in his *Life of King Arthur* had been unfavorable to its sale. Yet this was a work addressed to a class of persons who might be presumed to be peculiarly free from prejudices which affect so powerfully the semi-educated. Such a fact speaks stronger than volumes of dissertations as to the opposition which reform of spelling must overcome before it can meet with any sort of consideration at the hands of many.

But of these partial reforms, it is the one proposed by Webster that is most familiar to Americans, and perhaps to all English-speaking readers; for the storm which it raised was violent enough at one time to be felt in every land where our tongue was employed. Nor, indeed, has it so completely subsided that occasional mutterings of it are not even yet heard. The Websterian orthography, it is to be remarked, is found only in its primitive, unadulterated purity in the edition of 1828. All the dictionaries bearing other dates than that must be neglected by him who seeks to penetrate to the very well-head of this movement; for the author himself, or his revisers for him, bent before the orthographic gale, and silently struck out in later editions every method of spelling which the popular palate could not be brought to endure or inserted everything which it earnestly craved. No more than those who preceded him did Webster go to work upon correct principles, even when looked at from the point of view of a partial reform. One main defect pervading his plan was that it was an effort to alter the orthography partly according to analogy and partly according to derivation. He could not well do both, for they often conflicted. Further- more, he was often not consistent in the one and very often not correct in the other.

As far back as 1806 Webster had published an octavo dictionary of the English language. From that time for the next twenty years his attention was mainly directed to the compila- tion of such a work on a large scale. He soon found it necessary, he tells us, to discard the etymological investigations of his predecessors as being insufficient and untrustworthy. This they largely were, without doubt; but by way of remedying the defect, Webster devoted years to getting up a series of derivations which were more insufficient and untrustworthy still. In the process of doing this he made a study of some twenty languages, and formed a synopsis of the principal words in these, arranged in classes under their primary elements or letters. The results of this study were embodied in the dictionary of 1828, and the orthography was occasionally made to conform to it. Webster took a serene satisfaction in these new spellings; but it was upon his etymology that he prided himself. In his view, it furnished a revelation of the hidden mysteries of language and a solution of the problem of its origin. With his eyes intently fixed upon the tower of Babel, he probably never felt so happy as when he fancied that he had come upon the trace of some English word found in the tongues made use of in the courts of Nimrod or Chedorlaomer.

It is a hard thing to say of a work which has taken up no small part of the lifetime of an earnest student that it is of little value; but there is not the slightest doubt that nearly all of Webster's supposed philological discoveries were the merest rubbish. Necessarily, inferences based upon them in regard to the proper method of spelling are utterly unworthy of respect. The derivation, indeed, had at last to follow the fate which had overtaken certain portions of the new orthography. Its retention was a little too much for later revisers of the dictionary. These, in the edition of 1864, swept away at one fell swoop into the limbo of forgettable and forgotten things the fruits of twenty years of etymological study. Those conclusions, which in the eyes of the author had given him the key to unlock the hidden secrets of language, are no longer allowed to appear on the pages of the very work which perpetuates his name.

The changes of another sort, based upon analogy, which Webster introduced with the idea of making the spelling of words uniform, were liable to little positive objection. Some of them, in spite of violent opposition, have in this country more than held their own. The consequence is that in the case of a number of words in common use we have two methods of spelling flourishing side by side. This is a state of things which, it seems to me, every one who has the reform of our orthography at heart must contemplate with unqualified satisfaction. Not that Webster's proposed changes, even had they been universally adopted, would have gone to the real root of the evil. Far from it. At best they merely touch the surface and then only in a few places. But one effect they have produced. They have in some measure prevented us, and do still prevent us, from falling to the dead level of an unreasoning uniformity. By bringing before us two methods of spelling, they keep open the legitimacy of each. They expose to every unprejudiced investigator the utter shallowness of the arguments that are directed against change.

But slight as Webster's alterations were, they

met with the bitterest hostility at the time of their introduction. The love of little things is deeply implanted in the human mind. It is, therefore, perhaps not unnatural that the minor changes in spelling which he proposed should have met with attack far more violent than that directed against his tremendous etymological speculations. This culminated on the publication of Worcester's Dictionary, which in the matter of orthography followed a more conservative course. A wordy war arose, which lasted for years. Combatants from every quarter leaped at once into the arena. They were easily equipped for the contest, inasmuch as virulence was the main thing required. Intellect was not essential to the discussion, and knowledge would have been a death-blow to it. The war of the dictionaries, as it was called, is therefore of interest to us at this point of time, not for any principle involved in it, but as an illustration, pertinent at the present moment, of how earnestly, and even furiously, men can be got to fight for a cause they do not understand.

There is no doubt, indeed, that Webster laid himself open to attack. Perfect consistency is not to be looked for in this world; but the man who sets out to make a reform *in* English orthography as contrasted with a reform *of* English orthography cannot help being inconsistent. He will feel obliged to retain objectionable spellings. He will even feel obliged to authorize some that are inconsistent with his own principles, for the same reason that Moses tolerated divorce. It is the hardness of men's hearts, clinging to ancient abuses and unwilling to break up old associations, which will force the reformer to accept what he does not approve. Inadvertence, too, will add failures of its own to the contradictions involved in the very incompleteness of the scheme which has been adopted.

Both in respect to analogy and derivation, Webster did not carry out the principles he avowed. There were whole classes of words which he hesitated to change; at least, he did not change them. Of these half-measures, whether due to oversight or to doubt, one illustration will suffice. No man who seeks to make orthography etymologically uniform can have failed to notice the difference of spelling in the case of words derived from the compounds of the Latin *cedo*. Three end in *eed*, six in *ede*. As the digraph *ee* has practically the same sound always, the former termination seems to me preferable. But laying aside personal opinions in the matter, what sensible reason can be

253

given for writing *succeed* with *ceed* and *secede* with *cede*? Here was a glaring anomaly which could hardly have failed to escape Webster's attention. If the principle of analogy met with any consideration, this demanded to be removed, if anything did. But he was unequal to the occasion. In the edition of 1828 he spelled *exceed* with *ceed* and *accede* with *cede*, which every one does, to be sure, but which he personally had no business to do. In conformity with his avowed views, he was bound to make uniform the orthography of all the words which come from the Latin *cedo*. As he failed to do this, he subjected himself to the reproach of not having acted in accordance with his own principles.

The truth is that analogical spelling occupied a very subordinate position in Webster's mind. His work is mainly deserving of notice because, unaided, he chanced in some cases to secure success in spite of virulent opposition. Its chief value, indeed, lies in the fact that it has kept alive a feeling of hostility to the existing orthography of the English tongue; that it has saved many from paying a silly and slavish deference to the opinions of a not very well-informed lexicographer of the eighteenth century and his successors; that in the matter of spelling it has inculcated the belief that there is a test of reason and scholarship to be applied, and not a mere prescription based upon ignorance; and that by these means it has given to some a hope, to others a fear, to all a warning, that however long Philistia may cling to her idols, they will be broken at last.

It would be a great mistake, however, to assume that the feeling about the wretched condition of English orthography has been confined to professional reformers. From almost the very beginning the users of written speech have been conscious of the burden they were carrying. It has certainly lain heavily upon the hearts of many thinking men in the past, and unconsciously, perhaps, on the hearts of all. But this feeling has never been translated into successful action. In truth, men believed themselves hopelessly entangled in a network of anomalies and absurdities which hampered all intelligent proceeding. Out of it they saw no way of escape. This despairing attitude is plainly apparent in the comments of the dramatist Ben Jonson on what he terms our pseudography. In speaking of the digraph *ck* in certain words, he remarked that it "were better written without the *c*, if that which we have received for orthography would yet be contented

255

to be altered. But that is an emendation rather to be wished than hoped for, after so long a reign of ill custom amongst us."

Consent to be altered, the language never did voluntarily. There is nothing more absolutely false than the assertion sometimes made that it has been and still is slowly but steadily reforming the spelling of its own initiative. Of the usage of the past it requires peculiar ignorance —though of that the supply is unlimited—to make an assertion of this sort. Everything of the little which has been accomplished in the way of reform has been gained only after a bitter contest. Undoubtedly there has been a steady tendency to give exclusive recognition to one out of several spellings of a word and thereby produce absolute uniformity. But there has been no disposition to make the spelling better. Not infrequently the worst form has been selected. Any one who takes the trouble to compare the orthography of the seventeenth century with that now prevailing will have frequent occasion to observe how slight has been the tendency toward simplification; that when a choice has lain between different spellings, it is not unusual to have the more unsuitable one preferred; and that, as a consequence, the divergence between orthography

256

and orthoepy has increased instead of diminishing.

In truth, in this matter we have often gone
back not merely from the practice of the seventeenth century, but from the more rigid practice
of the eighteenth. In the second half of the
latter period Johnson's Dictionary settled the
standard. The changes which have taken place
since his time have all been haphazard. They
have been sometimes for the better; they have
as frequently been for the worse. Take, for
illustration, *catcall, downfall, downhill, bethrall,
miscall, overfall, unroll, forestall.* In Johnson's
Dictionary these appear as *catcal, downfal, downhil, bethral, miscal, overfal, unrol,* and *forestal.*
As might be expected, there was no consistency
in his treatment of the terminations found in
these words. While he spelled *downhil* with a
single *l,* he spelled *uphill* with two. While he
spelled *install* with two *l's,* he spelled *reinstal*
with but one. Contradictory usages of this
sort are liable to turn up anywhere in his work.
Reconcilable, for instance, appears in it with an
e after the *il; irreconcilable* without this vowel.
Naturally, arbitrariness of spelling of such a sort
tended much more to the complication of orthography than to its simplification. There
was sufficient love of uniformity in our nature

to reduce many of these variations to one form; but as a general rule the form selected has been the one which carried the largest number of unnecessary letters. Take, for instance, the word *fulness*, so spelled by Johnson. It is now often written *fullness*, after the analogy of *illness* and *smallness*. But there is no consistency even in this practice. No one, for illustration, now spells *forgetfulness* with two *l*'s, though that method was once not uncommon.

In fact, on no side has any rational principle been at work, or if it has shown itself, it has never been allowed to carry out fully the results at which it has arrived. Against the agencies which have tended to widen the gulf between orthography and orthoepy counteracting influences, indeed, have at times manifested themselves. Two measures, in particular, the language has unconsciously taken to lighten the load under which it has been staggering. One of them is a natural action on the part of the users of speech; the other, though a growth, partakes of the nature of an artificial device. Both, however, have exerted an appreciable influence in making the spelling indicate the sound. The first to be considered is very limited in its operations. In ancient days, when pronunciation was changed the spelling was changed in

258

order to denote it. With the petrifaction of the orthography this in time became generally impossible. Since, therefore, the spelling could not be altered to accord with the pronunciation, there sprang up a tendency to alter the pronunciation to accord with the spelling. Letters once unsounded came to be heard. Syllables previously crushed out of all recognition were restored to their full rights. These agencies never have exerted and never can exert influence on any large scale. Still, they have been operative in some degree and continue to be active. Accordingly, when the disposition manifests itself to bring about in such ways consonance between orthography and orthoepy, it is not worth while to make now any change in the spelling. A few examples will make this point perfectly clear.

Any one who compares the pronunciation given in the dictionaries at the beginning of the nineteenth century with that now sanctioned by similar authorities, will be struck by a number of instances in which a given word was once not pronounced in accordance with its spelling, but is so at the present time. Take, for illustration, *housewife*. A century and more ago its regularly authorized pronunciation was *huzzif*. This continues still. Much more commonly, however, each syllable which enters into the compound is heard exactly as it would be were it used separately. The older pronunciation has mainly died out in consequence of men learning the language more through the eye than the ear; though in this particular case the degradation of the word to *huzzy* has probably contributed its aid to produce the result.

Chart will supply us with another illustration. A century ago it was frequently pronounced *cart*. *Cognizance* and *recognizance*, too, have now taken up generally the sound of *g*, though in legal circles this letter still frequently remains suppressed. Take, again, the case of some words in which *qu* had once the sound of *k* as it is still heard in *etiquette* and *coquette*. Walker informs us that in his day *harlequin* and *quadrille* were pronounced *har-le-kin* and *ka-drill*. In both these instances, under the influence of the printed word, the *qu* has generally abandoned the sound of *k* for the regular sound which we ordinarily associate with this digraph. The same thing is going on in the case of *masquerade*. The dictionaries, which rarely record such changes till they have been fully accomplished, give us no intimation of this fact. This last observation applies also to *pretty*, in which *e* has regularly the sound of short *i*. But the disposition to give the vowel here its strictly proper sound is showing itself in the case of this word. If left to run its natural course, it is likely in time to become predominant.

As a general rule, however, words subject to influences of this sort are not likely to be those commonly heard in conversation. They belong to the class which are more usually met in books. There he who sees them for the first time is disposed to make the pronunciation accord as near as possible to the spelling. To this rule there are occasional notable exceptions. I have heard even educated men—at least, men who were generally so regarded—pronounce the words *English* and *England* just as they are spelled— that is, the initial syllable was sounded as *ĕng* and not as *ĭng*. No such pronunciation is ever likely to become common enough to bring itself into notice; but that it should exist at all is proof of how wide-reaching is the tendency just mentioned.

These words themselves, it may be added, are interesting illustrations of one of the various agencies which have done so much with us to bring about divergence between orthography and orthoepy. In our earlier speech there were two ways of denoting this initial syllable, corresponding, without doubt, to the two ways in which it was pronounced. In one case it was spelled *eng*, as it is now, in close accordance with its derivation. In the other case it was spelled *ing*, giving us, with the usual orthographic variations, the forms *Ingland* and *Inglish*. Here a genuine difference in sound conveyed to the ear was represented to the eye by a difference of orthography. The modern speech has made one of its usual compromises. It has retained the spelling of the one form and the pronunciation of the other. A similar story can be told of *colonel*, which had once as an allied form *coronel*. It is likewise true of *lieutenant*. In the case of this word, what is regular in the United States is exceptional in England, and vice versa. With us the pronunciation of the first syllable is almost universally in accordance with that of the simple word *lieu*, which is its original. In England it is not allowed to be contaminated by any sound which might indicate its derivation. From a by-gone spelling, *lef*, comes the pronunciation there prevalent. This has survived the form that created it.

But the most striking illustration of a change, mainly effected by the agency of the written word, is seen in the past participle *been*. There is little question—there is, indeed, no question—

that at the beginning of the nineteenth century, and even much later, the digraph *ee* in this word had in cultivated speech the sound of short *i*. It is not meant that the other pronunciation which rymed it with *seen* was not sometimes heard; but merely that it was then so limited in use that orthoepists hardly thought it worth while to recognize its existence. Walker admitted no pronunciation of *been* save that which made it ryme with *sin*. He had heard of the other, but he had only heard of it. So said Sheridan, his contemporary and rival. So said Smart, his reviser and successor, writing in the middle of the nineteenth century.[1] Yet, with no support from the most prominent lexical authorities, the pronunciation of *been* to ryme with *seen* instead of *sin*, steadily gained ground in England during the last century. There it seems to have become finally the prevalent one. To it the New Historical English Dictionary, while sanctioning both ways of pronouncing the word, gives the preference—at least, the apparent preference.

The growth of this practice has, without question, been largely and perhaps mainly due to the fact that the digraph *ee* has been practically

[1] Walker's Pronouncing Dictionary, revised by B. II. Smart, 5th edition, London, 1857, p. xxiii., sec. 119.

263

confined to the representation of a single sound. It has become to us a phonetic symbol, denoting almost invariably the so-called "long *e*." Having this sound in nearly every case, there is unconsciously developed the feeling that it ought to have it always. For the sake of conforming to it, *been* has in consequence steadily tended to abandon its once more common pronunciation. This single example is of special interest, because of the proof it furnishes of the unifying tendency that would be exerted over language were phonetic symbols with fixed values employed to represent one sound and but one sound. It does more than that. It indicates the only way in which permanence can be given to pronunciation.

Even now, so marked is the influence of the training of the eye as compared with that of the ear, that efforts consciously or unconsciously go on to modify the sound of the word as we have been accustomed to hear it to the form of it which we are accustomed to see. It is no unusual thing to hear persons painfully striving to pronounce the final *n* of *condemn*, *contemn*, and similar verbs, making themselves very miserable when they fail, and others very miserable when they succeed. But, after all, efforts to bring about in this way accord between form and

264

sound can affect only a very limited class of words. The gap between orthography and orthoepy is, with us, too wide and impassable for the latter ever to close up. The most we can do is in process of time to revive the pronunciation of a few letters that are now silent, or to substitute a few forms etymologically correct for the corruptions by which they have been supplanted. When either of these courses shows signs of immediate or even of ultimate adoption, it is not worth while to disturb the coming of that result by present attempts at alteration. But in its best estate the changes of pronunciation to accord with the spelling cannot, as regards influence, be compared with the much more ancient device now to be considered. This consists in appending an unpronounced *e* to the final syllable to indicate that the preceding vowel is long. This method early evolved itself out of the confusion in which our orthography was involved as a sort of help to denote the pronunciation by the spelling.

There seems to be something peculiarly attractive to our race in the letter *e*. Especially is this so when it serves no useful purpose. Adding it at random to syllables, and especially to final syllables, is supposed to give a peculiar old-time flavor to the spelling. For this belief there is, to some extent, historic justification. The letter still remains appended to scores of words in which it has lost the pronunciation once belonging to it. Again, it has been added to scores of others apparently to amplify their proportions. We have in our speech a large number of monosyllables. As a sort of consolation to their shrunken condition an *e* has been appended to them, apparently to make them present a more portly appearance. The fancy we all have for this vowel not only recalls the wit but suggests the wisdom of Charles Lamb's exquisite pun upon Pope's line that our race is largely made up of "the mob of gentlemen who write with ease." The belief, in truth, seems to prevail that the final *e* is somehow indicative of aristocracy. In proper names, particularly, it is felt to impart a certain distinction to the appellation, lifting it far above the grade of low associations. It has the crowning merit of uselessness; and in the eyes of many uselessness seems to be regarded as the distinguishing mark of any noble class, either of things or persons. Still, I have so much respect for the rights of property that it seems to me every man ought to have the privilege of spelling and pronouncing his own name in any way he pleases.

The prevalence of this letter at the end of

words was largely due to the fact that the vowels *a*, *o*, and *u* of the original endings were all weakened to it in the break-up of the language which followed the Norman conquest. Hence, it became the common ending of the noun. The further disappearance of the consonant *n* from the original termination of the infinitive extended this usage to the verb. The Anglo-Saxon *tellan* and *helpan*, for instance, after being weakened to *tellen* and *helpen*, became *telle* and *helpe*. Words not of native origin fell under the influence of this general tendency and adopted an *e* to which they were in nowise entitled. Even Anglo-Saxon nouns which ended in a consonant—such, for instance, as *hors* and *mús* and *stán*—are now represented by *horse* and *mouse* and *stone*. The truth is, that when the memory of the earlier form of the word had passed away an *e* was liable to be appended, on any pretext, to the end of it. The feeling still continues to affect us all. Our eyes have become so accustomed to seeing a final *e* which no one thinks of pronouncing, that the word is felt by some to have a certain sort of incompleteness if it be not found there. In no other way can I account for Lord Macaulay's spelling the comparatively modern verb *edit* as *edite*. This seems to be a distinction peculiar to himself.

How widely prevalent at one period became the use of this final *e* can be brought out sharply by an examination of a few pages of a single work. Take, for example, *The Schoolmaster* of Roger Ascham. This was published in 1570. In the admirable reprint of it, executed by Professor Arber, the preface occupies eight pages. In this limited space we find an *e* appended to no small number of words from which it is now dropped. It appears in the nouns *bargaine, beginninge, booke, daye, deale, deede, eare, feare, fructe* (fruit), *gowne, greife* (*sic*), *hinte, kinde, learninge, logike, minde, realme, rhetorike, silke, sonne, spirite, sworde, stuffe, taulke, wisdome, wonte,* and *worke;* in the verbs *beare, gatte* (preterite), *looke, passe, seeme, teache, thanke, thinke, tooke* (preterite), and *waulke;* in the adjectives *certaine, fewe, fitte, fonde, lewde* or *leude, lothe, meane, olde, poore, shrewde,* and *sweete;* and in the adverbs *againe, agoe, cheife* (*sic*), and *doune.* On the other hand, this final *e* is absent from some words where it is now regularly found. *Come* and *become,* for example, appear as *cum* and *becum,* and *tongue* as *tong.*

In the chaos which came over the spelling in consequence of the uncertainty attached to the sound of the vowels, the final *e* was seized upon as a sort of help to indicate the pronunciation. Its office in this respect was announced as early as the end of the sixteenth century; at least, then it was announced that an unsounded *e* at the end of a word indicated that the preceding vowel was long. This, it hardly need be said, is a crude and unscientific method of denoting pronunciation. It is a process purely empirical. It is far removed from the ideal that no letter should exist in a word which is not sounded. Yet, to some extent, this artificial makeshift has been and still is a working principle. Were it carried out consistently it might be regarded as, on the whole, serving a useful purpose. But here, as well as elsewhere, the trail of the orthographic serpent is discoverable. Here, as elsewhere, it renders impossible the full enjoyment of even this slight section of an orthographic paradise. Here, as elsewhere, manifests itself the besetting sin of our spelling, that there is no consistency in the application of any principle. Some of our most common verbs violate the rule (if rule it can be called), such as *have, give, love, are, done.* In these the preceding vowel is not long but short. There are further large classes of words ending in *ile, ine, ite, ive,* where this final *e* would serve to mislead the inquirer as to the pronunciation

269

had he no other source of information than the spelling.

Still, in the case of some of these words the operation of this principle has had, and is doubtless continuing to have, a certain influence. Take, for instance, the word *hostile*. In the early nineteenth century, if we can trust the most. authoritative dictionaries, this word was regularly pronounced in England as if spelled *hos'-tĭl*. So it is to-day in America. But the influence of the final *e* has tended to prolong, in the former country, the sound of the preceding *i*. Consequently, a usual, and probably the usual, pronunciation there is *hos-tīle*. We can see a similar tendency manifested in the case of several other adjectives. A disposition to give many of them the long diphthongal sound of the *i* is frequently displayed in the pronunciation of such words as *agile, docile, ductile, futile, infantile*. Save in the case of the last one of this list, the dictionaries once gave the *ile* nothing but the sound of *il;* now they usually authorize both ways.

Were the principle here indicated fully carried out, pronunciations now condemned as vulgarisms would displace those now considered correct. In accordance with it, for instance, *engine*, as it is spelled, should strictly have the *i* long. One of the devices employed by Dickens in *Martin Chuzzlewit* to ridicule what he pretended was the American speech was to have the characters pronounce *genuine* as *gen-u-īne*, *prejudice* as *prej-u-dīce*, *active* and *native* as *ac-tȳve* and *na-tīve*. Doubtless he heard such pronunciations from some men. Yet, in these instances, the speaker was carried along by the same tendency which in cultivated English has succeeded in turning the pronunciation *hos-tĭl* into *hos-tīle*. Were there any binding force in the application of the rule which imparts to the termination *e* the power of lengthening the preceding vowel, no one would have any business to give to it in the final syllable of the words just specified any other sound than that of "long *i*." The pronunciations ridiculed by Dickens would be the only pronunciations allowable. Accordingly, the way to make the rule universally effective is to drop this final *e* when it does not produce such an effect. If *genuine* is to be pronounced *gen-u-ĭn*, so it ought to be spelled.

For a long period, indeed, in the early history of our speech, whenever pronunciation changed, spelling was changed for the sake of denoting it properly. If a letter then became silent, it had no rights which any one felt bound to respect.

It was incontinently dropped. No one needs to be told that this has all been changed in modern times. With us it has become both the belief and the practice that if a letter has once got into the spelling of a word, no matter how unlawfully, it has acquired the right of remaining there forever. In consequence, our language is encumbered with a lot of alphabetic squatters which have settled down upon the orthography without any regard to the opposing claims of either derivation or pronunciation. The mental attitude which at first tolerated and at last has learned to love these nuisances sprang up after the invention of printing. The influence of this art upon the spelling is something that cannot well be overestimated. Any confusion which might before have existed in it became from this time worse confounded. Upon the introduction of printing, indeed, English orthography entered into the realm of chaos and old night, in which it has ever since been floundering. Then it began to put on the shape it at present bears, "if shape it may be called which shape has none."

The evil effects wrought on the orthography by printing, as contrasted with the previous method of manuscript reproduction, were largely due to the difference of conditions under which the two arts were carried on. The early type-setters, indeed, had to encounter the same difficulties which beset the copyists of manuscripts. There were among educated men the widest diversities of pronunciation. No established literary, still less established orthoepic standard, to which all felt obliged to conform, could possibly grow up during the long civil strife of the fifteenth century. Disorder and confusion, which in many cases had their origin as far back as the coming together in one tongue of two conflicting phonetic systems, continued to prevail to a great extent. But the copyists of manuscripts, compared with the type-setters who succeeded them, were men of education. Some degree of cultivation was essential to a profession which demanded as the first condition of success the ability to gain a clear conception of an author's meaning. In accordance with the practice then universally prevailing, they would give to the word the spelling which to them represented the pronunciation. As educated men, this would be done in the majority of cases with a reasonable degree of accuracy.

Still, that the copyists of manuscripts were a long way from reaching the highest ideal of excellence we know from incontestable authority. The corruption of the text caused by their

wilfulness or carelessness was one of the few
things that seem to have vexed the genial soul
of the first great singer of our literature. Chaucer
in his address to Adam, the scrivener, complains
of the great trouble to which he is put in re-
vising his works by the latter's negligence. A
fervent prayer is made that he may have a
scalled head if he does not hereafter adhere to
the original writing more closely. Toward the
end of *Troilus and Cryseyde* there is, as Mr.
Ellis remarked, something almost pathetic in
his address to his "litel boke"

> And for ther is so greet dyversitee
> In Englissh and in writynge of our tonge,
> So preye I God, that non myswrite thee,
> Ne the mys-metere for defaut of tonge.

It is not likely that either imprecation or
imploration had much effect upon the scribes
of that day, who were probably as perverse a
generation as the scribes of old. But one thing
is to be said in their behalf. The cardinal principle that the proper office of orthography is
to represent orthoepy they never lost sight of,
however wofully they may have failed in carrying it into effect. Had this been consistently
kept in view, the attainment of a reasonably
complete correspondence between spelling and

pronunciation, while it might have been long delayed, would have been sure to follow at last.

All this was checked and finally reversed by the introduction of printing. Far higher requirements, as has been intimated, were needed in the work of the copyist than in the mere mechanical labor of the type-setter. The former had to understand his author to represent correctly what he said. But there is no such necessity in the case of the compositor. Whatever intellect he may have, he will not be called upon to use it to any great extent in his special line of activity. His duty is done if he faithfully follows copy, and he can perform his work well in a language of which he does not comprehend a word. His labor is and must always be mostly mechanical. The very fact that he is not responsible for results will inevitably have a tendency to make him careless in details. The blunders in spelling, and in greater matters still, shown in modern printing-offices where the most scrupulous care is exerted to attain correctness are familiar to all. These evils would be immensely increased at a period when no such extensive precautions against error were taken in any case, and when in some cases it would seem as if no precautions were taken at all. The effects of the carelessness and in-

275

difference that frequently prevailed would not be and were not confined to the work in which they were directly manifested. The orthography of printed matter necessarily reacts upon the orthography of the men who are familiar with it. These, when they come to write, will be apt to repeat the errors they have learned from the books they read. With that peculiar ability in blundering shown by all careless spellers, they will further contribute numberless variations of their own. These in turn will be followed more or less by the type-setter. Thus, new forms will be constantly added to the prevailing disorder. In this manner a complete circle is formed in which author and printer corrupt each other, and both together corrupt the public.

Such was, in great measure, the situation of things in the sixteenth and seventeenth centuries. Differences of spelling in the same book and on the same page were found constantly. But necessarily it was a situation which could not continue. To a printing-office, uniformity of orthography, if not absolutely essential, is, to say the least, highly desirable. Toward uniformity, therefore, the printing-offices steadily bent their aim, since nobody and nothing else would. The movement in that direction was powerfully helped forward by the feeling, which had been steadily gaining strength after the revival of classical learning, that the office, or at least one great office, of orthography is to indicate derivation. Belief in this involved in its very nature the notion of fixedness of spelling. It therefore gave the sanction of a quasi-scholarship to the demand for an unvarying standard which came from a mechanic art. Under the pressing needs of the printing-office, the movement toward uniformity made steady progress during the seventeenth century and the first half of the eighteenth. Wide variations continued to be found in works bearing the imprint of different establishments. We must remember that there were then no dictionaries that men were disposed to consider authoritative. It was not until the eighteenth century that these began to exist on any scale worth mentioning, or that much respect was paid to the spellings they sanctioned. Each printing-office was largely a law unto itself.

But the desire for uniformity became more insistent as time went on. At last it succeeded in reaching the end it had in view. But unfortunately for us, the establishment of the orthography was in no way the work of scholars, though this was largely a result of their own

277

indolence and indifference. It came into the hands of men who knew nothing about it and cared still less. In consequence, it was a haphazard orthography that was fixed upon us. In the selections made by compositors and proofreaders from the variations of spelling which then prevailed, it was the merest accident or the blindest caprice that dictated the choice of the form to be permanently adopted. Authors themselves seem rarely to have taken any interest in the matter. The uniformity, or the approach to uniformity, we have now was accordingly the work of printers and not of scholars. As might be expected, the result of it is a mere conventional uniformity. In no sense of the word is it a scientific one. In effecting it, propriety was disregarded, etymology was perverted, and every principle of orthoepy defied. Men of culture blindly followed in the wake of a movement which they had not the power and probably not the knowledge to direct. Certainly they lacked the disposition. To the orthography thus manufactured Johnson's Dictionary, which came out in 1755, gave authority, gave currency—gave, in fact, universality. But it could not give consistency nor reason, for in it they were not to be found.

As a consequence of the wide acceptance of

this orthography, the petrifaction of the written speech which had been steadily going on for at least two centuries was now practically made complete. So far as the forms of the words were concerned, it assumed more and more the character of a dead language. But in the meanwhile the spoken tongue remained full of vigor and life. As a necessary consequence, it was constantly undergoing modification. While the spelling stood still, changes in pronunciation were numerous and rapid. Whether they were for the better or for the worse is not pertinent to this inquiry. But the inevitable result was to widen steadily the gulf that had long before begun to disclose itself as existing between the written and the spoken word. That result is before us. No particular value having been attached to any vowel or combination of vowels, there is nothing to determine the exact value they should have when they appear in a particular syllable. For the pronunciation we go not necessarily to the word itself but to somewhere else. Every member of the English race has to learn two languages, every member of the English race uses two languages. The one he reads and writes; the other he speaks.

CHAPTER VI

TWO languages, it has just been said, we have: one we write, and one we speak. To bring them even remotely into conformity is one of the hardest problems to solve that was ever put before the users of any tongue. It is manifest from the survey which was made of the orthographic situation, that the difficulties which stand in the way of reforming English spelling are not the difficulties which are ordinarily paraded. There are arguments against any change whatever. They do not seem to me strong ones, but they are honestly held. Furthermore, they are held by men who know too much about the language to be imposed upon by the cheap objections, which come from the unknowing or the unthinking. The only one of serious importance is the existence of that period of uncertainty and confusion which must attend the transition from the old to the new. This, to be sure, has

280

always existed to some extent. Once it existed to a great extent. It exists at the present day. The introductions or appendixes to our larger dictionaries contain lists of from fifteen hundred to two thousand words which still continue to be spelled in different ways. But many of these are not in common use. Hence, the number of them makes little impression upon the common mind.

But as no reform of any kind ever yet proved an unmixed blessing, so will not reform of English orthography. Especially will this be true of it at its introduction. A change of spelling on any large scale will involve for the time being certain disadvantages. The conflict between the old that is going out and the new that is coming in cannot fail to produce more or less of annoyance. These disturbances, indeed, last only for a time; but to some they are very real while they do last. Those of us who believe that the permanent benefits accruing to the users of our tongue from a reform of our orthography outweigh immensely the temporary inconveniences and annoyances to which they will be subject, can well afford to bear with the hesitation of those who like the end in view, but dislike the time and toil that must be gone through in order to reach it. There must always be taken into consideration the existence of a class of persons who look upon the present state of our orthography as an evil, but an evil that cannot be got rid of without costing more than the benefits received in return.

But such reasons for reluctance to unsettle the existing condition of things are widely different from the pretentious objections that are regularly advanced by those who have not studied the subject sufficiently to understand the real difficulties that lie in the way. Yet these imaginary obstacles loom up so large in the minds of many that they must receive a respectable amount of consideration, even if they are hardly entitled to respectful consideration. It is not for any value they have in themselves that they are discussed here. It is because they are constantly urged by men whose opinions on other subjects are frequently of highest value. The utter hollowness of these common objections to spelling reform will be shown in the course of the following pages, as well as the unconscious insincerity of those advancing them. I say unconscious, because the insincerity has not been caused by any attempt to ignore the facts or to conceal them. It is simply that these have never occurred to them. But I further say insincerity, because the moment the real facts are brought to their attention, they refuse to apply to particular cases the general principles upon which they have been loudly insisting. The further great difficulty in dealing with the honest objector does not consist merely in showing him that he is wrong in his facts. It is to make clear that his reasoning is wrong in the few instances in which his facts are right.

I

The first of these objections is connected with the subject of derivation. There goes on, we are told, an irrepressible conflict between etymological spelling and phonetic, or anything approaching phonetic spelling. If the latter come to occupy the foremost place, the former, it is asserted, will disappear. Incalculable harm would thereby be wrought both to the speech and to its speakers. According to some, life would become a burden to the individual, and the language would be ruined beyond redemption, if the spelling of a word should hide from our eyes the source from which it came. The mystic tie that binds the speech of the past to that of the present would be severed. This is the special argument which comes not unfrequently from members of the educated, and sometimes of the scholarly class, though not from that section of it which deals with English scholarship. In the course of the preceding pages there has been constant occasion to give illustrations of its falsity, and far too often of its fraud. Consequently, to discuss it directly and at length will seem to many very much like going through the process of slaying the slain. But it plays so conspicuous a part in all discussions of spelling reform, that it is perhaps advisable, if not necessary, to consider it with special fulness of detail.

There is no question, indeed, that this argument based upon etymology has the strongest hold upon the educated class. It is constantly brought forward as if it were sufficient of itself to settle the question. Words, we are told, have a descent of their own. Letters which are never heard in the spoken speech, and indeed cannot be pronounced by any conceivable position known to us of our vocal organs, are not to be dropped from the written speech, because they remind us, or at least remind some of us, of forms in the languages from which they originally came. It sends a peculiar thrill of rapture, we are assured, through the heart of the student to find, for illustration, in *deign, reign, feign,* and

284

impugn, a letter *g* which he never thinks of pronouncing.   Silent as it is to the ear, it is, nevertheless, eloquent with all the tender associations
connected with *dignor, fingo, regno,* and *impugno.*
That persons with little education, and on the
other hand persons with the highest linguistic
training, should not share in these feelings is not
at all to the purpose.   Such are not really the
ones to be consulted.   Between these two classes
lies a vast body of educated men whose wishes
in this matter should be considered paramount.

That this argument in their behalf may not
be charged with misrepresentation, take the
following passage from Archbishop Trench,
one of the deservedly favorite linguistic writers
of the previous generation.   Furthermore, as
about the only English scholar of any repute
who has come to the aid of the opponents of
spelling reform, his words deserve quotation
on that very account.   He is giving as a reason
for the retention of useless letters that while
they are silent to the ear, they remain eloquent
to the eye.   "It is urged, indeed," wrote Trench,
"as an answer to this, that the scholar does not
need these indications to help him to the
pedigree of the words with which he deals, that
the ignorant is not helped by them; that the
one knows without, and the other does not

know with them; so that, in either case, they are profitable for nothing. Let it be freely granted that this, in both these cases, is true; but between these two extremes there is a multitude of persons, neither accomplished scholars on the one side, nor yet wholly without the knowledge of all languages save their own on the other; and I cannot doubt that it is of great value that these should have all helps enabling them to recognize the words which they are using, whence they came, to what words in other languages they are nearly related, and what is their properest and strictest meaning." [1]

Now, in the first place, were all this true, the objection would not be a valid one. The well-being of the many is always to be preferred to the satisfaction of the few. A language does not exist for the sake of imparting joyful emotions to the members of a particular group who are familiar with its sources. When committed to writing it is so committed for the purpose of conveying clearly to the eye the sounds heard by the ear. Anything in the form of the printed word which stands in the way of the speediest arrival at such a result is to that extent objectionable. But even this so-called advantage

[1] *English, Past and Present*, p. 298, 8th edition, revised, London, 1873.

of suggesting origins is distinctly limited. What educated men know of the sources of words is almost entirely confined to Latin and Greek. Of the earlier forms of the more common native words and of their meanings the immense majority of even the most highly cultivated are ignorant. Their ignorance, however, does not seem to impair their happiness any more than it does their comprehension.

But the objection, further, is a purely artificial one. The happiness conferred is a happiness assumed to be confined to the words in their present form. The example of other tongues shows there is no justification for this belief. The Italian is a phonetic language. Does any one believe that an Italian scholar experiences any less satisfaction in finding the Græco-Latin *philosophia* converted in his speech into *filosofia* than an English one does in seeing it in the form *philosophy?* Has his language suffered any material injury in consequence? Were I not myself inconsistent and lazy and several other disreputable adjectives, I should write *fonetic* instead of *phonetic*. This I cheerfully admit. But were not the strictly virtuous defenders of spelling according to derivation equally lacking in consistency, and absolutely unfaithful to the high etymological ideals they hold up for our admiration, they would be writing *phansy*, at least, instead of *fancy*. In one of the sporadic attacks of common-sense which have sometimes overtaken the users of our speech, *f* has displaced *ph* in this word, though to prevent the result from being wholly rational it has substituted *c* for *s*. The Greek *phantasia* has come down to us through *phantasy*, *fantasy*, and has finally subsided into the present form. To the believer in etymological spelling *fancy* ought to be as objectionable as *fonetic*.

In the second place, the hollowness of this pretended regard for etymology is not only detected, it is emphasized by the fact that the opposition to change is equally pronounced in the case of words where the present form is the result of blundering ignorance which gives an utterly erroneous idea of their origin. Can any antagonist of simplification be induced by his devotion to derivation to abandon *comptroller?* This corrupt spelling does more than defy the pronunciation of the word; it gives an utterly false impression of its source. *Controller* is in Anglo-French *contre-rollour*, in law Latin *contra-rotulator*. These, again, were taken from the Latin *contra*, 'against,' and the diminutive *rotulus*, *rotula*, 'a little wheel,' which word in the middle ages acquired the meaning of 'roll.'

288

The controller, in consequence, was the one who kept the counter-roll or register, by which the entries on some other roll were tested. How naturally the possession of such an office would be apt to give to him holding it "control" over certain others, in the modern sense of the word, is apparent on the surface. But in the sixteenth century, and even earlier, some members of that class, "neither accomplished scholars on the one side nor yet wholly without the knowledge of all languages save their own on the other," got it into their heads that the first part of the word came from the French *compter*, 'to count.' Hence came the unphonetic spelling based upon a blunder of derivation.

Take two other examples, illustrative of this attitude of opposition. Could any upholder of etymological spelling be induced to drop the *c* of *scent*, though nobody ever pronounced the intruding letter? Yet, as it comes from the Latin *sent-ire*, the substitution of *scent* for the previous *sent* destroys in this case for the vast majority of educated men that delightful reminiscence of the classic tongues which, we are told, imparts so peculiar a charm to the present orthography. Mitford, the historian of Greece, was subjected to ceaseless ridicule and vitupera-

tion because he preferred the correct etymological form *iland*, and refused to adopt the *s*
which had been inserted into the word under
the blundering belief that it was either derived
from or was in some way related to the Latin
insula and the French *isle*.

In truth, the argument of derivation is invoked only to retain whatever orthographic
anomalies we chance to have. It is abjured the
moment an effort is made to root out any etymological anomalies which have been introduced
into the speech. The fact is that if spelling
according to derivation were heeded it would
result in changes to which those proposed by
any advocate of simplification of spelling would
seem absurdly trivial. This would be particularly noticeable in the case of words derived from native sources. The opponent of
spelling reform who bases his hostility upon
etymological grounds would be aghast were he
asked to conform to his principles in his practice.
Out indeed would go the *h* of the very word
aghast just used. Nothing would induce him
to drop the intruding letter in this case or other
letters in scores of other cases, though their
only effect is to hide the origin of the word.
Or take, for illustration of mere uselessness, the
k of whole classes of words of native origin.

The letter was as little known to the Anglo-Saxon alphabet as it was to the Roman.   Hence, were spelling according to derivation strictly enforced, it would have to disappear from no small number of words where it is not merely superfluous as regards pronunciation, but gives an entirely erroneous impression of the form from which it came.   It has been remarked that the original of *back* was *bæc*, of *quick* was *cwic*, of *stock* was *stoc*, of *sick* was *seoc*.   Imagine the indignant feelings of the assumed ardent devotee of spelling according to derivation if he were asked to drop the final letter from these words.   Yet from his own point of view it has no business there at all.

To a certain extent this particular brand of ruin had already overtaken the language. From the native words no one had ever thought of discarding the final *k*, because scarcely any one knew of the forms these originally had. But knowledge of Latin was widespread.   Regard for derivation succeeded, therefore, in banishing it from whole classes of words taken from that language.   The struggle, however, was long.   The authority of Doctor Johnson was in vain invoked for its retention.   One must be familiar with the history of orthography to appreciate what dissensions sprang up in once happy homes, what prognostics were indulged in of the ruin that would betide the speech, were men ever to be induced to spell *musick* and *historick* and *prosaick*, and a host of similar words, without their final *k*. Boswell, who could not help reproaching Johnson for dropping the vowel *u* from *authour*, praised him for standing up for the retention of this final consonant. He represents him as saying that he spelled *Imlac* in *Rasselas* with a *c* at the end because by so doing it was less like English, which, he continued, "should always have the Saxon *k* added to the *c*." The "Saxon k" was the lexicographer's personal contribution to the original English alphabet. "I hope," continued Boswell, "the authority of the great master of our language will stop this curtailing innovation by which we see *critic*, *public*, etc., frequently written instead of *critick*, *publick*, etc "

The biographer's hopes were doomed, however, to disappointment. Walker, the favorite lexicographer of a hundred years ago, bowed to the storm, while he deplored the havoc it had wrought. "It has been a custom within these twenty years," he wrote, "to omit the *k* at the end of words when preceded by *c*. This has introduced a novelty into the language, which is that of ending a word with an unusual letter, and is not only a blemish on the face of it, but may possibly produce some irregularity in future formations." To call it a novelty was stating the matter too strongly. But to this extent Walker's assertion was true, that spelling a word with a final *c* was only occasional.

Here we have been considering the dropping of a useless final letter which has no justification for its existence on the ground of derivation. This naturally leads to the consideration of the case in which it is proposed to drop a particular one which has such justification. This is the no longer pronounced guttural with which, as one example, *through* ends. One of the queer objections brought against the spelling *thru* was that hardly a word existed in our language that ended in the letter *u*. That seemed to the protester an all-sufficient reason for never letting any of them have that termination. If the sound was there to be represented, there seemed no very cogent reason why the letter fitted to represent it should not perform its office. In the original speech *u* terminated some most common words, as *sunu*, 'son'; *duru*, 'door'; and *pu*, 'thou.' What crime has this unfortunate vowel committed that it should be deprived of its ancient privilege of standing at the end of a word? The objection is interesting because it shows what sort of reasons intelligent people can be led to believe and to adduce under the honest impression that these are to be deemed arguments.

Another fallacy connected with this subject of spelling in conformity with the derivation is suggested by the extract taken from Archbishop Trench's work, rather than directly asserted in it. This is that a knowledge of the origin of words is a desirable if not an essential requisite to their proper use. Consequently, the spelling of the English word should be made to conform to the etymology for that particular reason. This is an assumption that has no warrant in fact. The existence of great authors in every literature, who had either no knowledge or had very imperfect knowledge of the sources of the speech which they wielded at will, is an argument which may be ignored, and ordinarily is ignored, because it can never be squarely met. It is not from their originals or from their past meanings that men learn the value of the terms they employ. Acquaintance with that comes from experience or observation, or from familiarity with the usage of the best speakers and writers. Is the meaning of *nausea* any plainer after we have learned that it is by origin a Greek word which come from *naus*, 'ship,' and in consequence ought strictly to be limited to

denoting seasickness? One hour's experience
of the sensation will give the sufferer a keener
appreciation and a preciser knowledge of the
signification than a whole year's study of the
derivation. Will *stirrup* be employed with
greater clearness after one has learned that in
the earliest English it was *stige-râp*, and that
accordingly it meant the 'rope' by which one
'sties' or mounts the horse? The information
thus gained has an independent value of its own.
It may be of interest as satisfying an intelligent
curiosity. It may show that the first stirrups
were probably made of ropes. But it implies
a mistaken and confused perception of what is
to be derived from etymological study, to fancy
that as a result of it any one will have a better
knowledge of this particular appendage to a
saddle or use the term denoting it with more
precision and expressiveness. It is only in the
exceptional cases, when a word is beginning to
wander away from its primitive or strictly proper sense, that the knowledge of the derivation
imparts accuracy of use. Yet even here this
knowledge is of slight value. The transition of
meaning is either a natural development which
ought not to be held in check, or it is a general perversion which the etymological training of the few is in most cases powerless to arrest.

One form of this fallacy of derivation is that which connects it with the history of words. The two are closely allied. They are, indeed, so closely allied that when one is spoken of, it is the other that is usually meant. We are often condescendingly assured by the opponent of spelling reform that its advocates forget that words have a history of their own. After indulging in this not particularly startling remark he almost invariably goes on to make clear by illustration that he himself has no conception of what it means. "Shall we," asks a writer, after reciting this well-worn formula— "shall we mask the Roman origin of *Cirencester* and *Towcester* by spelling them Sissiter and Towster," as they are pronounced? Now it may not be wise, for various reasons, to alter the orthography of proper names. But the unwisdom of it will not be for the reason here given. In this case it is evident from the words accompanying his protest that what the decryer of change means to say is that by altering the spelling of the place names, their history would be obscured. What he actually says, however, is that their derivation, which is but a single point in their history, would be hidden from view.

For the leading idea at the bottom of an argument of this sort, if it has any idea at all, must necessarily be that the particular form which the word assumed at the first known period of its existence should be the form religiously preserved for all future time. Now, if orthography is merely or, even mainly, to represent etymology; if, further, we are able both to obtain and retain the earliest spelling, there is method in this madness, even though there be not much sense. But of the first form we have been able to secure the knowledge with certainty in only a few instances. Far fewer are the instances in which we have retained it. Almost invariably it is a form belonging to some later period that is adopted and set before us as somehow having attained sanctity. This imputed sanctity works only harm. The maintenance of one form through all periods not only contributes nothing to the history of the word, it does all it can to prevent any knowledge of its history being kept alive. For it is the spoken word alone that has life. Only by the changes which the written word undergoes can the record of that life be preserved. If the written word remains in a fossilized condition, all direct knowledge of the successive stages through which the spoken word passed, disappears. The moment a word comes to have a fixed unchangeable exterior form, no matter what

297

alterations may take place in its interior life, that is to say, in its pronunciation, that moment its history, independent of the meaning it conveys, becomes doubtful and obscure. This is the condition to which English vocables are largely reduced. Their successive significations can be traced; but knowledge of the important changes of pronunciation they have undergone becomes difficult, if not impossible, of attainment.

Two terms designating common diseases may seem to illustrate fairly well the opposite condition of things here indicated. They are *quinsy* and *phthisic*. The one early dropped the forms *squinancy*, *squinacy*, and *squincy*, which belonged to the immediate Romance original. To that an *s* had been prefixed. When that letter ceased to be pronounced, no one thought of retaining it. So for that reason it disappeared from the English, just as for the opposite reason it has been preserved in the corresponding French word *esquinancie*. In this case a history has been unrolled before us. It is not unlike that seen in the supplanting of the form *chirurgeon* by *surgeon*. On the other hand, take the case of the word *phthisic*, as now ordinarily written. This form gives us no knowledge of the real history of the word. From other sources we learn that it was once spelled as it is now pronounced. The most current of several forms was *tisik*. In Milton it is found as *tizzic*. Such a spelling makes evident at once how it was then sounded, just as still do the corresponding *tisico* in Italian and *tisica* in Spanish. But in the seventeenth century, and even as early as the sixteenth, scholars went back to the Greek original and imposed upon the unfortunate word the combination *phth*, which by a liberal use of the imagination is supposed to have somehow the sound of *t*. This has finally come to prevail over the earlier phonetic spelling. He whose knowledge of the word is confined to its present form is almost necessarily led to believe that it was taken directly from its remote source. From all acquaintance with the various changes it has undergone, and with the pronunciation it has had at various periods, he is shut out. Archbishop Trench has pointed out the transition by which *emmet* has passed into *ant* through the intermediate spellings of *emet* and *amt*, which necessarily represented changes of sound.[1] By this means a history has been unrolled before us. But he certainly had no right to felicitate himself upon the result. If his theories be true, instead of spelling the word as we pronounce it,

---

[1] *English, Past and Present*, p. 326.

which we now do, we ought to adopt in writing the poetic and dialectic *emmet* at least, if not the earliest known form. To employ his own argument, letters silent to the ear would still be most eloquent to the eye. In this particular case some of us would be made happy beyond expression by being reminded of the Anglo-Saxon original *æmete*.

Even using history in the narrow and imperfect sense in which those who advance this argument constantly employ it, we are no better off. Nearly every old word in the language has had different forms at different periods of its existence. Which one of these is to be selected as the standard? When does this so - called history begin? Take the word we spell *head*. Shall we so write it because it is the custom to do so now? Or shall we go back to the Anglo-Saxon original *heâfod?* Or shall we adopt some one of its three dozen later forms —such, for instance, as *heved* or *heed* or *hed?* This last, which with our present pronunciation, would be a pure phonetic spelling, was more or less in use from the thirteenth to the eighteenth century. The reason for our preference for the existing form has no other basis than the habit of association to which attention has been so frequently called. We do not spell the word as *head* because it gives us a knowledge of the changes which have taken place in its history, for this it does not do at all. Nor do we so spell it because it gives us a knowledge of its derivation, for this it does very little. Nor further do we so spell it because it represents pronunciation, for this it does still less. We cling to it for no other reason than that we are used to it. What is here said of *head* can be said of thousands of other words.

Even in the case of Cirencester and Towcester, above mentioned, the same statement holds good. As there intimated, proper names do not really enter into the discussion of the general question. Being individual in their nature, they are more or less under the control of the individuals who own them. These can and do exercise the right of changing at will their orthography and their pronunciation. But for the sake of the argument, let us assume that it would be a gross outrage to spell the names of these towns as *Sissiter* and *Touster*. Let us admit that by such a change all knowledge of their Roman origin would be lost to those who did not care enough about it to make the matter a subject of special study. It is accordingly a natural and, indeed, a perfectly legitimate inference, that in the designation of towns the main office of

their orthography is to point out who founded
them or how they chanced to come into being.

If this be so, the principle ought to be carried
through consistently. What, in such a case,
should be done with *Exeter?* The ancient name
was *Exanceaster*, which passed through various
changes of form, among which were *Exscester*
and *Excester*. As early, at least, as the reign of
Queen Elizabeth it became usually *Exeter*. If
it be the object of spelling to impart information about the origin of places, ought we not
at any rate to return to the form *Excester*, to
remind "a multitude of persons, neither accomplished scholars on the one side, nor yet wholly
without the knowledge of all languages save their
own on the other," that the Romans once had
a permanent military station on the banks of
the Exe? It is to be feared that no devotion to
derivation would lead the inhabitants of the
city to sanction such a change. In truth, the
value of all knowledge of this sort is something
assumed, not really substantiated. The few
who need it, or wish it, can easily acquire it
without the necessity of perverting orthography
from its legitimate functions to the business of
imparting it. How many of the inhabitants
of Boston in Lincolnshire and of Boston in
Massachusetts lead useful, happy, and honored

lives, and go down to their graves in blissful unconsciousness of the fact that the name of their city has been shortened from Botolph's Town! How many of them are aware, indeed, that such a saint as Botolph ever existed at all?

In truth, all knowledge of the history of words ceases for most of us the moment these assume a fixed form, independent of the sounds they purport to represent. That history is found in the pronunciation. It is recorded and revealed to us only by the variations in spelling which variations in pronunciation require. In this matter the attitude of the past and of the present is distinctly at variance. Especially is this so in the case of unpronounced letters. Our ancestors discarded such without scruple, whether found in the original or not. We cling to them. We are not content with merely clinging to them. The more in the way they are, the more we cherish them. This point is brought out strikingly in the earlier and the later treatment of two initial letters which ceased to be sounded. These are *k* and *h*. The latter was incontinently dropped in writing when it failed to be heard in the pronunciation. This, indeed, was done so long ago that knowledge of the fact that the letter once existed at the beginning of certain words is now mainly confined to the students of our earlier speech. In the other case the unpronounced letter is still retained in the spelling. There is consequently no way for us to determine from the form of the word when this initial *k* ceased to be a living force. That knowledge must be gained with more or less of certainty from an independent investigation.

It has already been pointed out that there are some two dozen words in our speech in which an initial *k* followed by *n* is silent.[1] If the researches of Mr. Ellis can be trusted, the dropping of the sound of this letter from pronunciation in the speech of the educated took place in the seventeenth century. By that time English orthography was beginning to be subjected to that process of petrifaction which consummated its work in the century following. The external form in existence continued to be preserved with little or no modification, regardless of whatever changes took place in its internal life. Naturally these words beginning with an unpronounced *k* fell under this influence. Take as an illustration the word *knave*, corresponding to the German *knabe*, 'boy,' and having originally the same significa-

[1] See page 165.

tion. As regards its meaning the English word has passed through the successive senses of boy, of a boy as servant, of a servant without regard to age, of a rascally servant, and finally of a simple rascal with no reference to the time of life or the nature of employment. There it remains. The idea both of boyhood and of service has entirely disappeared. That of rascality, not at all implied in the original, has now become the predominant sense.

In the case of the signification, we have therefore a complete history unrolled before us. In the case of the form, we have but a partial history. It was not so at first. In the earlier period the spelling of the word changed with its pronunciation. The original was *cnafa*. The substitution of *k* for *c* indicated no difference in the sound. But the weakening of the final *a* to *e*, the replacing of *f* by *v* denoted the prevalence at the early period of the idea that the spelling was not designed to defy pronunciation, but to point it out. Then changes made in it are evidences of the changes that had been going on in the sound. But when later the *k* disappeared from the pronunciation, no attempt was made to indicate the fact by dropping it also from the spelling. By that time the printing-office had begun to fasten its fangs upon the language.

Consequently, the letter no longer heard by the ear was carefully retained to console the eye and burden the memory.

Now, it may not be advisable—at least, for the present—to discard the unpronounced initial letter in the case of words of this class; this, too, for reasons entirely independent of the feelings of association. The revival of the phonetic sense among the men of the English-speaking race is possible as a result of an extensive reform of English spelling. In that case the pronunciation of k before n might be resumed in English speech, just as it is still found in German. The letter, indeed, continues yet to be heard in English dialects, so that in one sense it has never died out. Highly improbable, therefore, as is the resumption of the sound, it is at least possible. This consideration, though it can not form an argument, may suggest a pretext for not discarding it at present. But to retain it on the ground of derivation is more than irrational in itself. It is absolutely inconsistent with the attitude which has been taken and is now universally approved in the case of words which once were spelled with an initial h.

Had the users of language been always under the sway of the feelings which have made us keep the k, no small number of common words which now begin with *l*, *n*, or *r* would have these letters preceded by the aspirate. So they were at first. This class may be represented by *ladder* and *lot*, the originals of which were *hlædder* and *hlot;* by *neck* and *nut*, originally *hnecca* and *hnut;* by *ring* and *roof*, originally *hring* and *hrôf*. The letter *h*, having disappeared from the pronunciation, our fathers dropped it from the spelling. The most ardent devotee of derivation as a guide to orthography would now be unwilling to restore it. The same men who would be horrified at the idea of dropping *k* from *knoll* and *knife*, because that letter or its equivalent is found in the original, would be equally horrified at the thought of restoring *h* to *loud* and *nap* and *raven*, though in all of them it once flourished. It is simply another illustration of the same old sham of invoking derivation to resist any change in the spelling to which we are accustomed, and of disregarding it, and even defying it, when we are asked to carry out our professed principles by altering the spelling so as to bring it into accordance with them.

II

There is still another objection to be considered. We are given to understand that difference of spelling is quite essential to the recognition of the meaning of words pronounced alike. Otherwise there would be danger of misapprehension. This is a point upon which Archbishop Trench insisted strongly. He discovered that great confusion would be caused by writing alike words which have the same sound when heard, but are distinguished to the sight. Such, for illustration, are *son* and *sun*, *rain* and *reign* and *rein*. This is one of those difficulties which are very formidable on paper, but nowhere else. It is what comes to men of learning from looking at language wholly from the side of the eye and not at all from that of the ear. In the controversy that went on in this country in consequence of the President's order, I noticed that in a certain communication an old friend of mine specified me personally as one setting out to destroy what he called sound English by arranging letters in a totally different way, and thereby seeking to reconstruct the language to its destruction. Naturally, he was indignant at the nefarious attempt, though had he stopped to consider the disproportion between the pettiness of the puny agent and the massiveness of the mighty fabric, there would have appeared little reason for much excitement. Personally, so far from feeling resentment at his words, I read them with even more amazement than sorrow. The argument he used is of the sort which I expect to find communicated to the press by that noble army of the ill-informed who are always rushing to the rescue of the English language from the reckless practices of those who do not use it with their assumed accuracy or spell it according to their ideas of propriety. But here the objection came from a real scholar.

His words were, therefore, a convincing argument for the necessity of reform. They revealed in a striking way the bewildering effect our orthography exercises over the reasoning powers. He wanted to know what the phonetists—they deserve that name, he told us—are going to do with words alike in sound but different in sense. He began with *ale* and *ail*. It might have been inferred from his argument that, unless *ail* and *ale* were spelled differently, no person could ever be quite certain whether he were suffering from the one or partaking of the other. Another of his instances was *bear* and *bare*. Does anybody, on hearing either of these words, hesitate about its meaning? Why should he, then, when he sees it, even if both were spelled the same way? Or again, take the noun *bear* by itself. If any one comes across it, does he suffer much perplexity in ascertaining whether it is

309

the bear of the wilderness or the bear of Wall Street that is meant?

This last example, indeed, exposes of itself the utter futility of this argument. There is an indefinite number of words in the language which have precisely the same form as nouns or verbs. The fact that they belong to different parts of speech never creates the slightest confusion. Furthermore, there are but few common words in the language which are not used in different senses, often in many different senses, sometimes in widely different senses. Does that fact cause any perceptible perplexity in the comprehension of their meaning? Do reporters, who must arrive at the sense through the medium of the ear, experience any difficulty in ascertaining what the speaker is trying to say? Does any one in any relation of life whatever? When a man is returning from a voyage across the Atlantic, is he bothered by the different significations of the same term when he is trying to ascertain whether it is his duty to pay a duty? When one meets the word *piece*, does he suffer from much embarrassment in determining whether it means a part of something, or a firearm, or a chessman, or a coin, or a portion of bread, or an article of baggage, or a painting, or a play, or a musical or literary composition?

SPELLING REFORM

Does any one experience trouble, on hearing a sentence containing the word *thick*, in determining whether it is an adjective or a noun, or whether it denotes 'dense,' or 'turbid,' or 'abundant,' or a measure of dimension? Given the connection in which it is employed, does any one mistake *rain* for *reign* or *rein?* The negative answer which must be made to such questions as these disposes at once of a difficulty that has no existence outside of the imagination.

In fact, language presents not merely many examples of words with the same spelling which have different meanings, but sometimes of those that have exactly opposite meanings. Yet that condition of things produces no confusion. Does any one hesitate about what course to pursue when told, on the one hand, to "stand fast" or on the other to "run fast?" Does he ever in actual life confound the word *cleave*, when it means to adhere with the *cleave* which means to destroy adherence by splitting? When you dress a fowl, you take something off it or out of it; when you dress a man, you put something on him. Or take an example which may fairly be considered as presenting a certain obscurity at the first glance. In his ode on the morning of Christ's Nativity,

Milton tells us that " Kings sate still with awful eye." Here *awful* does not have the sense, most common with us, of ' inspiring awe,' but the strictly etymological one of ' full of awe.' Yet no one proposes to indicate by difference of spelling a difference of signification, the ascertainment of which depends not on the sight but on the brain. In truth, if no trouble is experienced in determining the meaning of words sounded alike in the hurry of conversation, when the hearer has but a moment to compare the connection and comprehend the thought, it is certainly borrowing a great deal of unnecessary anxiety to fancy that embarrassment could be caused in reading, where there is ample opportunity to stop and consider the context and reflect upon the sense which the passage must have. The actual existence of any such difficulty would imply an innate incapability of comprehension which, were it even justified by the individual consciousness of the asserter, it would be manifestly unfair to attribute to the whole race.

It needs but a moment's consideration to perceive the worthlessness of this argument. Yet let us put ourselves in the place of those who advance it, and treat it as if it had some weight. Let us assume that if words having the same pronunciation are spelled alike, a confused apprehension would be produced in the reader's mind. But are these believers in man's impenetrable stupidity willing to carry out the doctrine they profess to its logical conclusion? For the sake of preventing this assumed confused state of mind, are they willing to change the spelling of words which have precisely the same form but a pronunciation distinctly different? It will be found that the very men who clamor for the retention of different spellings for words pronounced alike are just as insistent upon the retention of words with similar spellings which are pronounced unlike. Of these there is a very respectable number in our tongue. Especially is this true of verbs and substantives which have precisely the same form on paper, but a different pronunciation. We *lead*, for example, an expedition to discover a *lead* mine. A *tarry* rope may cause us to *tarry*. This inconsistency of attitude is necessarily more marked in words belonging to the same part of speech. In consequence, a burden is imposed upon the learner of mastering a distinction which, in a language sensibly spelled, would be ashamed to put in a plea for its existence. *Slough*, 'a miry place,' has as little resemblance in sound as in meaning to *slough*, 'the cast-off skin of a

313

serpent.' We indicate the *tear* in our eyes and
the *tear* in our clothes by words which have
little likeness of sound, but have the same spelling in the written speech. We could go on
enumerating examples of this sort; but to
what end? It is maintained, according to the
theory enunciated in the case of *ail* and *ale*,
that a distinction of form in these and similar
words ought to be insisted upon so that the
reader may discover without effort which one
is meant. But the application of this very
argument would be at once scouted were an
attempt made to extend the principle to words
spelled alike but pronounced differently. This
is but another of the numberless inconsistencies
in which the opponents of reform find themselves plunged when they attempt to stand up
for the existing orthography on the ground of
reason.

III

So much for an objection which, if not serious
in itself, has to many a serious look. There has
been another brought forward which is so base-
less, not to call it comic, that nothing but the
sincerity of those adducing it would justify its
consideration at all. It is to the effect that,
were there any thorough reform of the spelling,

all existing books would be rendered valueless. Owners of great libraries, built up at the cost of no end of time and toil and money, would see their great collections brought to nought. The rich and varied literature of the past could no longer be easily read; it would have to wait for the slow work of presses to transmit it to the new generation in its modern form. Such is the horrible prospect which has been held before our eyes. The view would be absurd enough if directed against thoroughgoing phonetic reform. But as against the comparatively petty changes which are proposed and which alone stand now any chance of adoption, language is hardly vituperative enough to describe its fatuousness. But as in the discussion of this question we have to deal largely with orthographic babes, it is desirable to pay it some slight attention.

For the purpose of quieting the fears which have been expressed, it is necessary to observe that change of anything established, even when generally recognized as for the better, is not accomplished easily. Therefore, it is not accomplished quickly. It never partakes of the nature of a cataclysm. For its reception and establishment it requires regular effort, not impulsive effort; it requires labor prolonged as well as patient. It took, for instance, many scores of years to establish the metric system wherever it now prevails, with all the power of governments behind it. When the change made depends upon the voluntary action of individuals it must inevitably be far slower. Any reform of spelling in English speech which is ever proposed must stretch over a long period of years before it is universally adopted. There will consequently be ample time for both publishers and book-owners to set their houses in order before the actual arrival of the impending calamity.

This is on the supposition that it can be deemed a calamity to either. There is actually about it nothing of that nature. The process deplored is a process which is going on every day before our eyes. There is not an author of repute in our literature of whose works new editions are not constantly appearing in order to satisfy a demand which the stock on hand does not supply. Few, comparatively, are the instances in which a classic English writer is read in editions which came out during his lifetime. This is true even of those who flourished as late as the middle of the last century. How many are the people who read Thackeray, Dickens, and Macaulay in books which appeared before the death of these authors? If there is any de-

mand for their works, these are constantly reprinted and republished. But the appearance
of the new book does not lower the value of
the old, if it be really valuable. If it be not,
if the edition supplanted is of an inferior character or has been merely a trade speculation, it
has already served its purpose when it has paid
for itself. Under any conditions it can be
trusted to meet the fate it deserves.

So much for the point of view of booksellers
and book-owners. As regards book-readers,
the fear is just as fatuous. Few, again, are the
men who read works of any long repute—naturally the most valuable works of all—in the
spelling which the author used who wrote them
and in which the publisher first produced them.
It is not because the difference in this respect
between the present and the past breeds dislike.
On this point the book-market furnishes incontrovertible testimony. Valuable works which
are printed in an orthography different from
that now prevailing do not decrease in price at
all. On the contrary, they steadily rise. This
is a fact which the impecunious student, in
search of early editions, learned long ago, not to
his heart's content, but to its discontent. The
increase in value renders them difficult for him
to procure. Does the difference of spelling

render them difficult to decipher? A single example will suffice to settle that point. At the present moment there lies before me the first edition of the greatest English satire to which the strife of political parties has given birth— the *Absalom and Achitophel* of John Dryden. It was published in November, 1681. To purchase it now would, under ordinary circumstances, take far more money than it would to buy the best and completest edition of the whole of Dryden's poems. It consists of ten hundred and twenty lines of rymed heroic verse. The number of different words it contains may be guessed at from that fact; it has never, to my knowledge, been determined. But the words which are spelled differently in it from what they are now are just about two hundred.

This first edition itself presents certain characteristics of spelling so alien to our present orthography that it suggests that those now desiring change in it need not necessarily be put to death as having plotted treason against the language. In truth, the examination of this one poem, as it originally appeared, would destroy numerous beliefs which ignorance has created and tradition handed down and superstition has come to sanctify. A few of the facts found in it may be worth recounting for the benefit of those who fancy that forms now prevailing have descended to us from a remote past. Among the two hundred variations from the now prevalent usage are the past participles *allowd, bard, confind, coold, enclind, faild, shund, unquestiond,* and *banisht, byast, impoverisht, laught, opprest, pact, puft, snatcht.* We have also *red* as a preterite and *sed* as a participle. Further, not only is *could* most frequently spelled *coud,* which is etymologically right, but there also appears *shoud,* which is phonetically nearer right but is etymologically wrong. *Woud,* indeed, is distinctly preferred to *would,* the former being found ten times, the latter but once. *Monarch* occurs as *monark, mould* as *mold, whole* and *wholesome* as *hole* and *holsom.* *Scepter* is also the form found, and not *sceptre.* In the case of several words there are still not unfrequent those variant spellings which were common before the printing - house had established our present uniformity, or, rather, approach to uniformity. There is variation in the *or, our* forms with, on the whole, a distinct preference for the latter, as might have been expected when the influence of the French language and literature was predominant. *Labor,* for instance, as a noun or verb, occurs full two dozen times. In every instance it is spelled *labour.* So also in the same way are found *authour, emperour, inventour, oratour, superiour, successour, tutour,* and *warriour.* Not the slightest hint of these and such like facts can be gathered from editions now current. This single illustration brings out strongly the practice of the modern publisher in printing the writings of the great authors of the past, not in the orthography they themselves employed but in that which recent custom has chosen to set up in its place. Still, with all these differences just mentioned, and others not specified, the most unintelligent opponent of spelling reform would experience no difficulty whatever in reading the poem.

IV

Another objection remains to be considered. It is not really directed against any proposals made by any organized bodies which have taken up the consideration of the subject. These, to use the distinction already specified, devote themselves to reform *in* English orthography and not to reform *of* it. This latter is the object aimed at by individuals and not by societies. Consequently, this objection does not strictly concern the plans for simplification now before the public. It is really directed against the

far wider-reaching reform which would aim to
render the spelling phonetic. It is regarded
by some as so crushing that I have deferred its
consideration to the last. It may be summed
up in a few words. Variations of sound are
almost numberless. They cause a marked
difference of pronunciation among individuals,
a more marked difference between different
parts of the same country. Furthermore, they
are often so delicate as almost to defy representation. You could not denote them if you
would; and if you could, you would be encumbered, rather than aided, by the multiplicity of
signs. It is impossible, therefore, to have our
tongue spelled phonetically, because it is pronounced differently by different persons equally
well educated. Whose pronunciation will you
adopt? That is the point which has first to be
determined. It is safe to say that it is one
which can never be determined satisfactorily.
That fact is of itself decisive of the matter in
dispute.

This view of the question at issue is triumphantly put forward as one which can never
be successfully met. Assuming for the sake of
the argument that it is a genuine objection, let
us look at what it involves. The very result of
the lawlessness of our present orthography is

given as the reason why no attempt should be made to bring it under the reign of law. It is a real maxim in morals, and a theoretical one in jurisprudence, that an offender has no right to take advantage of his own wrong. This is the very course, however, which opponents of change recommend for adoption. Our orthography has rendered the orthoepy varying and doubtful. No one can tell from the spelling of a word how it ought to be pronounced. The result is that it is pronounced differently by different men. Accordingly, there should be no attempt to reduce the orthography to order, because the uncertainty which has been fastened upon it by the pronunciation has rendered it impossible to ascertain what it really ought to be.

But it never seems to occur to those who advance this argument that difficulties of the sort here indicated are not experienced in languages which for all practical purposes are phonetically spelled, such as Italian and Spanish. Even German can be included, because its variations from the normal standard do not extend to the great source of our woes, the arbitrary and different sounds given to the vowels and combinations of vowels. But take, for example, the first mentioned of these tongues. Its pronunciation differs in different parts of the country.

SPELLING REFORM

In some cases the variation is very distinctly
marked. Yet, while the spelling remains the
same, no embarrassment follows of the kind indicated. If this simple fact had been taken into
consideration, it would at once have disclosed the
nature of the imaginary strength and actual
weakness of this supposedly crushing argument.

For of all the hallucinations that disturb the
mental vision of the advocates of the existing
orthography, this is perhaps the most dismal
as it is the most unreal. No phonetically spelled
tongue ever has or ever would set out to record
the varying shades of the pronunciation of any
country, still less the varying shades of the pronunciation of individuals. A system which
indicates the delicate distinction of sounds
characterizing the speech of different regions
resembles the chemist's scales, which detect the
variation in weight of filaments of hair to all
appearance precisely alike. Instrumentalities
of this nature phoneticians may need and use
in order to represent the slightest diversities
of pronunciation. They can and do get up for
their own guidance characters conveying differences even of intonation. But these the ordinary speaker does not require at all. Instead
of benefiting him, they would be in his way.
For the average man, even of highest cultiva-

tion, it is no more important that shades of
pronunciation should be denoted in his alphabet than it would be important for him to lug
about in all temperatures and in all climates
an astronomical clock with a compensation pen-
dulum. What any working phonetic system
would set out to do is to give those broad and
easily recognizable characteristics of educated
utterance which are sufficient to indicate to
the hearer what the speaker is aiming to say.
It would represent a norm sufficiently narrow of
limit to make understood what is said, and sufficiently broad to offer within justifiable bounds
ample opportunity for the play of individual
or territorial peculiarities. Its principal effect
would be to set up a standard which would be
ever before the eyes of men.

In truth, the comparison just made is sufficient
of itself to lay this ghastly specter of an argument which haunts so persistently the imagination of many opponents of phonetic spelling.
It is with our pronunciation as with our time-
pieces. None of our watches run precisely
alike. Few if any can be called unqualifiedly
correct. For all that, with the aid of these
imperfect and never precisely agreeing instru-
ments, we manage to transact with little friction
and delay the daily business of a life in which

we have constantly to wait upon one another's movements. So, in the matter of sounds, a phonetic alphabet would denote only those clearly recognizable distinctions which are apparent to the ear of ordinary men. Orthography based upon such an alphabet would assume as the very foundation upon which to build itself the existence of a recognized standard orthoepy. It is that alone which the spelling would represent. Provincial speakers in consequence would have always before their eyes in the form of the word its exact and proper pronunciation. By it they would be able to compare and if necessary to correct their own.

But we may be told that while a standard time actually exists, a standard pronunciation does not. Consequently, no phonetic spelling can be established which will be regarded by any large portion of the general public as satisfactory. The all-sufficient answer to this objection is that the very thing which it is said cannot be done has been already done and done many times. It has been done, too, in the face of the very objection that it could not be done at all. The proof of this statement lies in the existence of the pronouncing dictionary. Works of this nature did not appear until the latter part of the eighteenth century. Before they appeared the project of producing them was criticised with extreme severity. They were denounced as irrational of nature and as impossible of execution. The same arguments, assumed to be convincing, were produced against them as those just considered against uniform phonetic spelling. Doctor Johnson brought the artillery of his ponderous polysyllables to bear upon them. He proved—at least, to his own satisfaction—the utter futility of Sheridan's scheme of preparing a work of this nature. His argument was based entirely on the ground of the wide differences prevailing in pronunciation. In spite of these arguments pronouncing dictionaries were prepared. At a comparatively early period several appeared in rapid succession. They are now so thoroughly established in the affections of us all that were a dictionary to leave out this characteristic it would cease to have consideration and sale. But a work of such sort goes upon the assumption that there is a standard pronunciation. Otherwise it would have no justification for its own existence. Its compilers seek to ascertain and represent this standard. A word, indeed, may be and not unfrequently is pronounced differently by different classes of educated men. In that case both or all sounds of it will be rec-

ognized—at least, until such time as one has
come to prevail over the other or over all others.
The pronouncing dictionary was indeed a
necessity of the situation. It was called by
Archbishop Trench "the absurdest of all
books." On what ground it can be called
absurd by an advocate of the existing orthography it is hard to determine. It is, without
doubt, a clumsy substitute for phonetic spelling.
It is not for him, however, who protests against
such spelling to denounce the aid to correct
pronunciation, imperfect as it may be, which
has been rendered absolutely essential by the
general prevalence of the beliefs he accepts and
defends. Had pronouncing dictionaries not
come to exist, the divergence which has been
going on between spelling and pronunciation in
consequence of our lawless orthography would
have rapidly extended with the extension of the
language and with the increasing number of
those who came to speak it, dwelling as they do
in regions far apart. Diversities of pronunciation would have been sure to spring up in such
a case even among the educated classes, to say
nothing of those prevailing in classes of different
social grades living almost in contact. As a
matter of fact such do spring up now. They
must necessarily continue to spring up in a lan-

guage where the spelling is not under the sway of phonetic law. But they are reduced to the lowest possible terms, in consequence of the wide use of pronouncing dictionaries. Between the authorizations of these there are at times divergences, but the agreements are far more numerous than the divergences. Hence, the authorizations are sufficient to keep the language fairly uniform. Furthermore, these works bring out clearly the truth of the statement with which this chapter began: that every speaker of English has to learn two languages. In dictionaries, the one he reads and writes is given the place of honor on the printed page. To it he turns whenever for any purpose he wishes to consult its meaning. Following after it, whenever the word is not itself phonetically spelled, is the form of it, usually in parentheses, as it is heard from the lips of men. To this he turns for its pronunciation.

No project is entertained by any organized body to establish phonetic spelling. It can hardly be said to exist outside of dictionaries. These have to employ it or some approach to it in order to convey to the users of language a conception of the proper pronunciation which the form itself does not indicate. The discussion of the subject is, therefore, an academic ques-

tion rather than a practical one. But this it is
desirable to say about it. Phonetic spelling is
not a destructive but a conservative agency.
Just as the creation of literature holds a language fast to its moorings, just as it renders it
stable by arresting all speedy verbal or gram-
matical change, so the establishment of phonetic spelling would operate upon orthoepy.
The exact pronunciation would be imposed upon
the word by its very form. No one could mistake it, no one would be tempted to disregard it.
From it there would never be variation save when
a change in the sound imperatively demanded a change in the spelling to indicate it. This
is a counsel of perfection which we can recognize
as desirable, but need never expect—at least, in
our day—to see realized. None the less can we
discern the benefits that would result from it.
Had it existed with us, the wide degradation of
that sound of *a* which is represented in *father*
and *far* could not have gone on at the rapid rate
it has done in this country. There are districts
in the United States where even the following
l does not protect it, and *calm*, for illustration, is
made to ryme with *clam*. Did phonetic spelling exist in the mother country, the pronunciation of *a* almost like "long *i*"—as, for example,
late, which by American ears is apt to be mis-

329

taken for *light*—now so prevalent in London and apparently extending over England, could never have held its ground, even with those who had received but a limited education. With an orthography which has no recognizable standard of correct usage, degradations of this sort are always liable to occur; nothing, in fact, can keep them from occurring.

CHAPTER VII

THERE remains one final consideration. No one who has had the patience to ex-examine dispassionately the facts contained in the preceding chapters can have failed to recognize the loss of time and waste of effort which the acquisition of our present orthography involves. Beside these, the needless squandering of money it causes, though a subject of just complaint, seems to me, after all, of slight account. But even evils of this sort, great as they unquestionably are, yield in importance to one far greater. In truth, it is not because of the waste of time in education—harmful as that unquestionably is—that our present orthography is peculiarly objectionable. It is the direct influence the acquisition of it exerts in putting the intellectual faculties to sleep at the most active period of life. Learning to spell is, with us, a purely mechanical process. As a mental discipline it is as utterly valueless as mere memorizing, where the student does not un-

331

derstand what he is repeating. Like that, it is also a positive intellectual injury. At the very outset of his school life the child is introduced into a study in which one natural and most important process in education, that of reasoning from analogy, is summarily suppressed. He finds at once, because the sound in one word is represented in one way, that it does not follow, as it ought, that in the next word he comes to it will be represented the same way. On the contrary, he finds it denoted by an entirely different combination of letters for no reason which he can possibly discover. It accordingly never enters his head that a sign, whether consisting of a single letter or a digraph, represents a particular sound and strictly ought never to represent but one. For him it can and usually does represent any one of half-a-dozen. This of itself tends to deprive him of the possession of all knowledge of the number and value of the sounds belonging to our speech. Unfortunately such a result is not the worst. The far more serious injury caused is the influence exerted upon the mind by the prohibition which the acquiring of our present orthography succeeds in imposing upon the exercise of the reason.

We can get some glimpse of the havoc

332

wrought to the reasoning powers by considering a single one of hundreds of illustrations that could be cited. At the very outset of his study the child is given, for example, the words *bed* and *red* to spell. If he has been properly trained up to this point, the limited acquaintance he has made with the values of letters leads him to say *b-e-d* and *r-e-d*. These are pure phonetic spellings. They satisfy all the conditions. Then he is introduced to the word *head*. Reasoning from analogy, he proceeds to spell it *h-e-d*. But here authority steps in and directs him to insert another letter for which neither he nor his instructor can see the use. Then the word *bead* is shown him. Following the analogy of *head*, he naturally pronounces it *bĕd*. Once more authority steps in and directs him to give the combination *ea* another and quite distinct sound. Next, he is presented with the infinitives and presents, *read* and *hear*. Conforming to the example just given, and perceiving it to be satisfactory, he fancies that he has reached at last a secure haven. He finds his error when he meets the preterites of these two verbs. Both have the same vowel combinations as the present. One of them has precisely the same form. But he discovers that *read* of the preterite has quite a distinct pronunciation from *read* of the present,

333

and that the *ea* of *heard* has still another sound, distinct from that of either, to which he has not yet been introduced.

This condition of things is one which in numerous cases cannot easily be remedied, owing to the lawlessness prevailing in our representation of sounds. For the present, therefore, it may have to stand. But let us take up one or two cases where irrationality now prevails, and yet where a rational change can be made easily. It would, for instance, assuredly seem hard for a being who possesses intellect enough to be lost or saved to pretend that he sees any reason why the plural of words ending in *o* should end sometimes with simple *s* and sometimes with *es*. Occasionally they have both terminations, according to the fancy of the individual writer. For illustration, the plurals of *grotto*, *halo*, *memento*, *motto*, and *negro* are spelled by some authors with *os* and by others with *oes*. In the case of *hero*, the latter ending has become the one regularly employed. This is probably due to the fact that the singular once ended in *e*. Discarded from that, it has transferred its unnecessary existence to the plural. As the large majority of these words never had the *e* as a termination, there seems not to be the slightest excuse on the ground either of derivation or pronunciation for

334

inserting anywhere in the inflection the un-necessary letter. On the other hand, there seems every reason for making the spelling of the termination of this class of words uniform. Yet men will be found to insist in imposing upon the learner the task of mastering a distinction which serves no other purpose than to defy analogy and insult common sense.

Or take another sort of trouble which adds its burden to early education and contributes its share to the impairment of the reasoning powers. In the case of certain words the child is censured if he leaves a letter out. In the case of other words of precisely the same character and origin he is censured if he puts it in. He is asked, for example, to spell the conjunction *till*. The men who first employed the word had no use for but one *l*. They therefore did not double it. Now if the child spells it, as did his remote ancestors, with a single *l*, he is blamed; but when he comes to its compound *until*, he is blamed again if he spells it with two *l*'s. If such differences of form served any purpose whatever, some justification might be pleaded for their maintenance. But nothing of the sort do they do. They simply heap up the burden of useless or rather harmful knowledge with which children are compelled to load their memory in defiance

335

of their reason. Time which should be spent in learning something valuable in itself, and therefore permanently profitable, is now wasted in mastering empty distinctions in the external representation of words which have no distinction in reality, but are reckoned conventionally of the first importance.

Is it any wonder that in circumstances like these the child should speedily infer that it is of no benefit to him to make use of what little reasoning power he has been enabled to acquire? He must force himself to submit blindly to authority, which compels him to accept as true what he feels to be false. Now, authority in education is a good as well as a necessary thing when its dictates are based upon reason. But when they are not, when in truth they are defiant of reason, no more pernicious element can well enter into the training of the young. Doubtless the logical processes employed in other studies correct in time for most of us the mental twist thus imparted in childhood. But it is not always corrected. We have only to read certain of the arguments advanced against spelling reform to become aware that the faculty of reasoning on this subject which has been muddled in childhood is apt to remain muddled the rest of one's life.

336

SPELLING REFORM

One illustration will bring out pointedly the truth of this last assertion. There is frequent complaint that the children in our schools spell badly. In this there is nothing new. It is a charge which has been made in every generation since spelling assumed the abnormal importance which has been imparted to it by modern devotion. In the sense in which it is often understood the complaint has no foundation in fact. Children spell just as well now as they did a generation or generations ago. If anything—persons of different periods, but belonging to the same class being alone taken into consideration—the proportion of so-called good spellers will pretty certainly be found larger now than ever before. But there always has been, and so long as our present absurd orthography continues there always will be, a goodly number of persons by whom it will never be thoroughly acquired. By many a respectable mastery of it will not be gained till a comparatively late period in their education. All this, too, in spite of the fact that in the popular mind correctness of spelling has assumed an exceptional importance. A man can blunder in his statement of facts; he can lay down false premises and draw from them the absurdest conclusions; he can exhibit incompetence and

337

inconsequence in the discussion of matters important or unimportant—yet none of these gross manifestations of ignorance and incapacity will bring him so much discredit in the eyes of many as the inability to spell certain common words properly. There is something even worse than this. In many communities a man may be a drunkard or a libertine with far less injury to his reputation than the disclosure of the fact that he is unable to spell correctly.

This state of feeling has imparted to spelling a factitious importance in modern education. But it involves further an inconsistency in the course of many of the stoutest defenders of the present orthography. These are often seeking to reconcile things which are incompatible. No more frequent attacks are made upon the system of education prevalent in our higher institutions of learning than the stress they are supposed to lay upon the cultivation of the memory instead of the reason. Now, if there be any truth in this accusation, the course adopted is nothing more than an extension to the advanced student of the very processes which are used in the instruction of the child. In learning to spell, his memory is developed not merely in place of the reason, but too often in defiance of it. Yet in nineteen cases out of twenty it will

SPELLING REFORM

be found that the very persons who indulge in the most lugubrious lamentations about the subordination of the reason to the memory in the educational processes employed in our universities, are the ones who insist most strongly upon the retention of an orthography which tends inevitably to produce the very effect they profess to deplore. In one breath they complain of the poor spelling of the students in our schools and colleges. In the next breath they object to any alterations which would bring order where now all is inconsistency and confusion; to changes of any sort which would make English orthography approach nearer rationality, and, therefore, easier to acquire. Is it not fair to consider this attitude on their part a direct result of that mental twist already mentioned as imparted in childhood?

I do not believe myself that the English race, once fully awakened to the exact character of English orthography, will cling forever to a system which wastes the time of useful years, and can only exhibit as its best educational result the development of the memory at the expense of the reasoning powers. I do not underrate the immensity of the obstacles which lie in the path of those who set out to accomplish even the slightest change. There is, first and

339

foremost, the impossibility of effecting, in the present state of public opinion, any thorough-going and therefore completely consistent reform. In any partial reform which can be secured there will be certain to remain inconveniences and inconsistencies which it must be left to the future to correct. At these the objector can always plausibly carp. But there is something more than the difficulty inherent in the matter itself. This is the immensity of the efforts demanded to destroy the superstition as to the sanctity of this creation, not of scholars, but of printers, which we call English orthography. Even to do this preliminary work will require the time and toil of years of struggle.

The fact is perhaps not much to be regretted. There is nothing worth living for that is not worth fighting for. But the task is no light one. Not merely have ignorance and prejudice to be overcome, but, what is far worse, stupidities, against which, the poet tells us, even the gods fight unvictorious. The higher class of minds have, indeed, been largely gained over. But there is little limit to the endeavor that must be put forth before any impression can be made upon that inert mass which prefers to remain content with any degree of error, however great, in preference to making any attempt to correct it, however slight. Still, this is the usual experience of all movements which aim to overthrow "the reign of ill custom"—to use Jonson's words—which has long prevailed. The advocates of reform of English orthography can expect nothing different. But they can be encouraged by the recollection that the efforts of men in the past engaged in even harder enterprises have after long years of struggle been carried to successful completion, because the combatants themselves have been sustained by the hope, and have acted under the inspiration, that what ought to be is to be.

VERBAL INDEX

about, *adv.* and *prep.*, 77.
accede, *v.*, 254.
acre, aker, *n.*, 26, 27.
active, *a.*, 271.
æcer, *n.*, 27.
æra, *n.*, 122.
æther, *n.*, 122.
after, *prep.*, 101.
again, *adv.*, 119.
aghast, *a.*, 177, 290.
agile, *a.*, 270.
ah, *interjec.*, 170.
ail, *v.*, 309, 314.
aile, *n.*, 87.
aisle (aile, ile, yle), *n.*, 77,
   126, 137, 181.
ale, *n.*, 87, 309, 314.
allowd, *p.p.*, 319.
ambassador, -our, *n.*, 197,
   212, 221.
amphitheater, -re, *n.*, 31.
anchor, *n.* and *v.*, 178.
annual, *a.*, 130.
annuity, *n.*, 130.
answer, *v.*, 101, 172.
ant, *n.*, 299.
anterior, -our, *a.*, 211.
antique, *a.*, 105.
antre (antar, antree), *n.*,
   34.
any, *a.*, 119, 120.
archangel, *n.*, 186.

archbishop, *n.*, 186.
are, *v.*, 79, 269.
asafœtida, *n.*, 152.
author, -our, *n.*, 206, 213,
   220, 223, 292, 320.
autumn, *n.*, 168.
awful, *a.*, 312.
aye, *adv.* and *n.*, 77.
ayther (either), *a.* and
   conj., 146.

back, *n.*, 171, 220, 291.
balm, *n.*, 102.
banisht, *p.p.*, 319.
bar, *n.* and *v.*, 102.
bard, *p.p.*, 319.
bare, *a.*, 309.
bath, *n.*, 102.
bead, *n.*, 333.
bear, *n.* and *v.*, 309.
become, becum, *v.*, 268.
bed, *n.*, 333.
been, *p.p.*, 124, 136, 262–
   264.
bethral(l), *v.*, 257.
"bile," *v.*, 134.
billet, -doux, *n.*, 169, 181.
blood, *n.*, 132, 153.
Boston, *n.*, 302.
Botolph, St., *n.*, 303.
bow, *n.*, 169.
break, *v.*, 115.

VERBAL INDEX

breeches, *n.*, *pl.*, 124, 136.
broad, *a.*, 114.
build (bild, byld), *v.*, 124.
builded, built, *p.p.*, 184.
bullock, *n.*, 171.
burn, *v.*, 105.
business, *n.*, 124.
busy, *a.*, 124.
but, *adv.* and *conj.*, 105.
buy, *v.*, 77, 126, 157.
byast, *p.p.*, 319

cag, *n.*, 120.
calf, *n.*, 102, 103, 162.
calm, *a.*, 102, 329.
candor, -our, *n.*, 212.
canoe, *n.*, 152.
caprice, *n.*, 105.
car, *n.*, 102.
catcal(l), *n.*, 257.
catch, *v.*, 120.
center,-re,*n.*, 28, 30, 31, 33.
centry, *n.*, 29.
centure, *n.*, 29.
chance, *n.* and *v.*, 101.
chart, *n.*, 260.
check, cheque, *n.*, 159.
chirurgeon, *n.*, 298.
choir, *n.*, 77, 186.
Cirencester, *n.*, 296, 301.
clamor, -our, *n.*, 231.
cleave, *v.*, 311.
clerk, *n.*, 113.
climb, clime, *v.*, 165, 166.
cognizance, *n.*, 260.
college, colledge, *n.*, 188.
colonel, *n.*, 262.
color, -our, *n.*, 196, 206, 228.
comb, *n.*, 165, 166.
come, cum, *v.*, 268.
complete, compleat, *a.*, 121.

compt, *n.* and *v.*, 163.
comptroller, *n.*, 162, 188.
conceit, conceipt, *n.* 180.
condemn, *v.*, 168, 264.
condemnation, *n.*, 168.
confessor, -our, *n.*, 197.
confind, *p.p.*, 319.
congratulate, *v.*, 102.
conspirator, -our, *n.*, 220.
contemn, *v.*, 264.
controller, *n.*, 162, 288.
convey, *v.*, 8.
coold, *p.p.*, 319.
coquette, *n.*, 260.
coronel, *n.*, 262.
coud(e), *pret.*, 179, 319.
cough, *n.*, 77, 156.
could, *pret.*, 179, 319.
count, *n.* and *v.*, 162.
critick, *n.*, 292.
critique, *n.*, 105.
crum, crumb, *n.*, 167.
cupboard, *n.*, 183.
czar, *n.*, 165.

dance, *n.* and *v.*, 101.
danger (dainger), *n.*, 87.
debit, *n.*, 173.
debt, det, *n.*, 5, 172.
deceit, *n.*, 8, 180; deceipt, 180.
deign, *v.*, 8, 284.
diameter, *n.*, 8.
diocese, diocess, *n.*, 60–68.
disdain, *v.* and *n.*, 8.
docile, *a.*, 270.
doctor, -our, *n.*, 220.
does, *v.*, 132.
done, *p.p.*, 269.
door, *n.*, 127, 153, 293.
doubt, dout, *n.*, 5, 172.
downfal(l), *n.*, 257.

344

345

VERBAL INDEX

grotto, *n.*, 334.
guage, *v.* *See* gage.
guard, *n.* and *v.*, 113.
guardian, *n.*, 113.
guild, *n.*, 124.
guilt, *n.*, 124.
guy, *n.*, 157.

ha, *interj.*, 170.
haddock, *n.*, 171.
hale, *a.*, 15.
half, *n.* and *adv.*, 102, 103.
hallelujah, *n.*, 170, 183.
halo, *n.*, 334.
hammock, *n.*, 171.
harlequin, *n.*, 260.
hassock, *n.*, 171.
haunch, *n.*, 113.
haunt, *n.*, 113.
hautbois, *n.*, 181.
have, *v.*, 269.
havoc, havock, *n.*, 171.
head, *n.*, 300, 333.
heal, *n* , 15.
health, *n.*, 17.
hear, *v.*, 333.
heard, *pret.* and *p.p.*, 334.
hearken, *v.*, 113.
heart, *n.*, 113.
hearth, *n.*, 144.
hed, heed, *n.*, 300.
heifer, *n.*, 119, 145.
height, *n.*, 77, 126, 145.
heir, *n.*, 114.
hero, *n.*, 334.
heved, *n.*, 300.
hexameter, *n.*, 8.
high, hye, *a.*, 182.
hillock, *n.*, 171.
historick, *a.*, 292.
hole, *a.*, 15, 319.
hol(e)some, *a.*, 319.
honnour, *n.*, 234.

honor, *n.* and *v.*, 5, 8, 194–237.
honorable, honourable, *a.*, 8, 203.
honorary, *a.*, 8.
horror, -our, *n.*, 221, 231.
hostile, *a.*, 270.
hot, *a.*, 14, 15.
hour, *n.*, 198.
housewife, *n.*, 259.
humor, -our, *n.*, 195, 203, 205, 232.
huzzy, *n.*, 260.
hymn, *n.* and *v.*, 168.

iland, *n.*, 290.
impoverisht, *p.p.*, 319.
impugn, *v.*, 285.
infantile, *a.*, 270.
Ingland, *n* , 261.
Inglish, *a.*, 262.
innovator, -our, *n.*, 220.
instal(l), *v.*, 257.
interior, -our, *a.*, 211.
intrigue, *n.*, 105.
inveigh, *v.*, 8.
inventor, -our, *n.*, 320.
irreconcil(e)able, *a.*, 257.
island, *n.*, 181.
isle, *n.*, 181.

jail, *n.*, 115, 116.
jeopard, *v.*, 119.
jocose, *a.*, 26.
joke, *n.*, 26.

kay, *n.*, 141.
keg, *n.*, 120.
kennel, *n.*, 120.
"ketch," *v.*, 120.
key, *n.*, 122, 145.
key (quay), *n.*, 141, 142.
kiln, *n.*, 168.

346

VERBAL INDEX

348

VERBAL INDEX

349

VERBAL INDEX

GENERAL INDEX

a, as in *fare*, represented by *ai*, by *ay*, by *e*, by *ei*, 114.
"*a*, broad," 109, 136; represented by *au*, by *aw*, by *o*, by *oa*, 114; by *ou*, 114, 156.
"*a*, long," an *e* sound, 103, 114; represented by *ai*, by *ay*, by *ea*, by *ei*, by *ey*, by *e*, by *ao*, by *au*, 115.
a, long, represented by *ua*, by *ea*, by *e*, by *au*, 113.
a, short, represented by *ua*, by *ai*, 114.
a, sounds of, 100–103, 104, 106; weakened to *e*, 267; represents short *e*, 119, 120; represents short *o*, 126.
Academies, influence of, 59.
Addison, Joseph, 30, 31, 137.
ae, digraph, disappearance of, 122, 123; represents "long *e*," 122.
ai, digraph, represents *a* of *fare*, 136; "long *a*," 115, 136; "long *i*," 77, 126,137; short *e*,119,136.

Allen, Grant, 117.
Alphabet, for what invented, 73; English, 76; insufficiency of Roman, 97, 99, 107.
American spelling, so-called, 18, 25–29, 32.
Analogical spelling, 251, 254, 332–334.
Anglo-French words, 234, 288.
Anglo-Saxon, 27, 150, 175, 267, 291, 300.
ao, digraph, represents "long *a*," 115.
Arber, Edward, 151, 268.
Armstrong, John, 216, 217, 220.
Arnold, Matthew, 59–70.
Ascham, Roger, 127, 151, 268.
Association, sentiment of, 10–16, 20, 35, 36.
Ash, John, 228.
au, digraph, represents, "broad *a*," 114; "long *a*," 115; long *a*, 113.
aw, digraph, 109, 136; represents "broad *a*," 114.
ay, digraph, represents *a* of *fare*, 114; "long *a*," 115, 140; "long *e*," 122,

351

GENERAL INDEX

i, letter and sound, 97, 104, 105, 106; represents "short *u*," 132.
"*i*, long," a diphthong, 105, 133, 159; sound of represented by *ai*, by *ay*, by *ey*, by *i*, by *uy*, by *y*, by *ye*, 77; by *ei*, 77, 126; by *ie*, 77, 149; by *oi*, 77, 134; by *ui*, 158.
i, short, represented by *e*, 123, 124, 260; by *ee*, 124, 136, 262–264; by *ie*, 124; by *o*, 124; by *u*, 124; by *ui*, 124; by *y*, 123.
ie, digraph, represents "long *e*," 122, 149; "long *i*," 77, 126, 149; short *i*, 124; "short *u*," 132.
ieu, represents *ef*, 262; long *u*, 129.
ile, ending, 269, 270.
ine, ending, 269, 271.
Italian language and orthography, 49, 201, 287, 322.
ite, ending, 269.
ive, ending, 269, 271.

j, sounded as *y*, 183.
Johnson, Samuel, 64, 65, 102, 123, 127, 137, 145, 205, 207–214, 218, 219, 220, 221, 222, 223, 227, 228, 244, 254, 257, 278, 326.
Johnston, William, 155.
Jonson, Ben, 127, 255.
Journal des Débats, 61.

k, letter and sound, 26–

28, 97, 163, 170, 171, 172, 260, 290, 291–293, 303–306.
Kenrick, William, 155.
Kersey, John, 205.
Knowles, James Sheridan, 66.

l, letter and sound, 172, 179, 257, 258, 262, 335.
Lamb, Charles, 266.
Landor, Walter Savage, 225–227.
Latham, Robert Gordon, 68.
L'Estrange, Roger, 115.
logue, words ending in, 158.

m, letter, 162.
Macaulay, Thomas Babington, Lord, 267, 316.
Manley, Mrs., 87.
Martin, Benjamin, 605, 205.
Metric system, 55.
Middleton, Conyers, 217.
Millar, Andrew, 217.
Milton, John, 144, 225, 299, 312.
Minsheu, John, 64.
Mitford, William, 289.
Moore, Thomas, 191.
Morris, William, 191.
Müller, Max, 91.

n, letter and sound, 165, 264.
Nares, Robert, 146, 155.
ng, digraph, 185, 186.
Normandy, dialect of, 115.
Northern English dialect, 144.
Notes and Queries, 236.

GENERAL INDEX

355

GENERAL INDEX

356

GENERAL INDEX

THE END